D1626552

FINDING FAITH

FINDING FAITH

Andrew Knowles

A LION MANUAL

Text copyright © 1983 Andrew Knowles
This edition © Lion Publishing 1994

The author asserts the moral right
to be identified as the author of this work

Published by
Lion Publishing plc
Sandy Lane West, Oxford, England
ISBN 0 7459 2649 5
Lion Publishing
850 North Grove Avenue, Elgin, Illinois 60120,
USA
ISBN 0 7459 2649 5
Albatross Books Pty Ltd
PO Box 320, Sutherland, NSW 2232, Australia
ISBN 0 7324 0811 3

First edition 1983
This revised edition 1994

A catalogue record for this book is available
from the British Library

Library of Congress CIP Data applied for

Printed and bound in Malaysia

CONTENTS

THE BIG QUESTIONS

Alone under a starry sky or lounging in a dole queue or losing a loved one, sooner or later we will have to ask, and answer, the Big Questions:

Who am I?

Where am I?

Why am I?

Is there a God?

If thou hearest that a mountain has moved, believe it. But if thou hearest that a man has changed his nature, do not believe it.

MUSLIM PROVERB

I am fearfully and wonderfully made.

THE PSALMIST

Man is the only animal that blushes—and the only animal that needs to!

MARK TWAIN

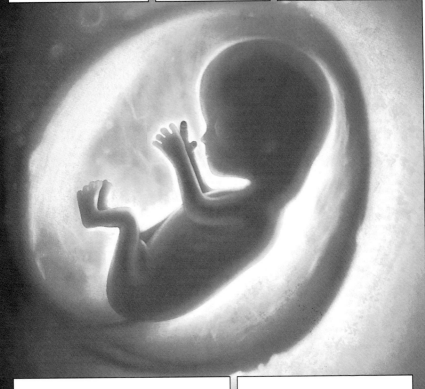

MAN (Homo sapiens) is a species of the sub-family Homininae of the super-family Hominoidea of the sub-order Simiae (or Anthropoidea) of the order Primates of the infra-class Eutheria of the sub-class Theria of the class Mammalia of the sub-phylum Vertebrata (Craniata) of the phylum Chordata of the sub-kingdom Metazoa of the animal kingdom.

GUINNESS BOOK OF RECORDS

Then God said, 'And now we will make human beings; they will be like us and resemble us. They will have power over the fish, the birds, and all animals, domestic and wild, large and small.' So God created human beings, making them to be like himself.

THE BOOK OF GENESIS

Who am I?

I am a mystery.

I wake up in the morning. I find myself the sole occupant of a complex, sensitive, and extremely useful body. I am also the proud owner of an intricate, imaginative, and highly resourceful brain. Everything about me is unique: my face, my finger prints, my 'self'.

I am alive. I develop. I grow. So does a vegetable. But I am more than a vegetable. Vegetables don't fall in love, or read the paper, or go on holiday...

I am a body with a brain; an animal. But—I am more than an animal. Animals don't peer through telescopes, or send birthday cards, or play chess, or cook...

The chemist tells me I am composed mostly of water, and contain quantities of carbon, calcium, and salt.

The biologist classifies me as Homo sapiens—a species of the sub-family Homininae filed among the Primates...

Where am I?

The astronomer tells me I am a speck on the face of a medium-sized planet spinning round a middle-aged star. The star, 'our' sun, is just one of a thousand million million million stars in a universe seventeen thousand million years old.

I feel small. I feel lonely.

Why am I?

Am I really a random coincidence, adrift in a cosmic accident, meaning

A human is nothing but:

- Fat enough for seven bars of soap
- Iron enough for one medium-sized nail
- Sugar enough for seven cups of tea
- Lime enough to whitewash one chicken coop
- Phosphorus enough to tip 2,200 matches
- Magnesium enough for one dose of salts
- Potash enough to explode one toy crane
- Sulphur enough to rid one dog of fleas

PROFESSOR C.E.M. JOAD

nothing, going nowhere?

Surely I have a dimension that animals and vegetables lack? After all, a carrot is oblivious of the size of Jupiter. A cow cares nothing for the speed of light.

But I am in a different class. I observe and appreciate. I create and choose. I am aware. I criticize. Sometimes I even criticize myself!

I am different. I am 'humankind'. In fact the Bible says I am 'Godkind'.

The Bible tells me that I am 'like God'; that I exist in something of the way that God exists, that I am aware in some of the ways that God is aware.

And although I cannot prove it, the idea that I am made in the image of God makes more sense than all the other views put together. Indeed, it helps me to put the other views together, and see them, and myself, as a whole.

I am a person created by God unique in the entire universe and in the whole of history and I know it!

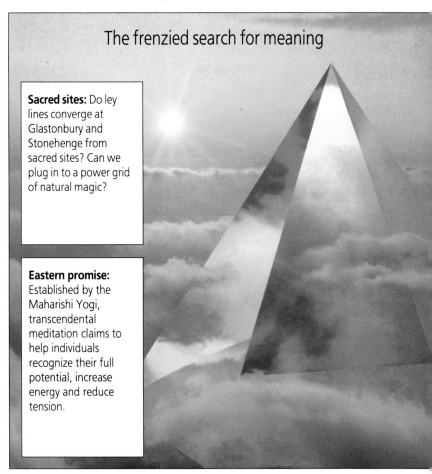

The frenzied search for meaning

Sacred sites: Do ley lines converge at Glastonbury and Stonehenge from sacred sites? Can we plug in to a power grid of natural magic?

Eastern promise: Established by the Maharishi Yogi, transcendental meditation claims to help individuals recognize their full potential, increase energy and reduce tension.

Is there a God?

Lots of people believe in God. But are they right?

When people say they believe in God, they normally mean one of two things: they have a vague belief that there is a power and purpose behind the universe. Someone or something has set it up, wound it up, and left it to run down. Or they believe there is some kind of life force that keeps everything going— a deep breathing and steady heart- beat sustaining the cosmos. Both sets of people would claim to believe in God, but neither would recognize the God of the other! One weaves God into the whole fabric of creation, while the other has a God which is entirely separate, disinterested, and eternally in the distance.

So what can we believe?

It is in fact impossible to prove that God exists through step-by-step

In the stars: Some say that the stars have a direct influence on human life and fate. Whatever the scientific basis for astrology, or lack of it, many people read their horoscopes every day.

Near-death experiences: Many people who have been very close to dying say that they emerged from a dark tunnel into a presence of joy and light. Scientists differ over the possible reasons for this, but those who have been through the experience are deeply influenced by it.

argument. If there was such a proof, it would have been discovered long ago, and no one would be in the slightest doubt!

But while there is no knock-down proof that an all-powerful, personal and loving God exists, there are many pointers in that direction. These are some of them:

Most astronomers now accept the theory that the universe had an instant of creation. It came to birth in a vast fireball explosion fifteen or twenty billion years ago. This is commonly known as the 'Big Bang' theory. Now, if there was a Beginning, could it be that there was a Beginner? The opening words of the Bible are: 'In the beginning, God created the universe...'

The universe is a place of majestic harmony and breath-taking variety. On our own planet, life is changing and developing all the time. Now if there is Design, could it be that there is a Designer?

Intelligent life as we know it has come about remarkably 'early' in the history of the universe. The odds against it happening were vast—'like an explosion in a printing works producing Shakespeare'! Unless, of course, it was intended...

Our world has built-in standards. The animal world is guided by instinct, but human beings enjoy free will, balanced by conscience. Why do we value goodness and truth? And how do we account for love? Even those who have never known what it is to love, or be loved, still know they are missing something.

Belief in God

The Christian and Jewish belief is that God *does* exist, and that he is a personal Creator. He exists quite independently of his creation, and yet he is intimately involved with it and concerned about it.

This means that the universe is not an accident. It is the work of a supremely powerful, intelligent and creative Being. Indeed, the sheer facts of creation, in all its vastness and variety, are the basic evidence God has given us to show that he exists.

It means that God is personal. It is he who has implanted qualities of goodness and love. The Bible pictures him as like a shepherd, caring for his people at all times and in every way. He is a Father, wanting the very best for his children; respecting their free will, yet providing a moral framework within which they can develop and grow.

2
ENTER JESUS

By any reckoning Jesus was amazing.
Born in Bethlehem, raised in Nazareth, and
executed just outside Jerusalem, Jesus never left
the pocket handkerchief of a country then called
Palestine. He left no writings or diaries, and all we
know of him could have been said and done in the
course of a few weeks. Yet Jesus' words and
actions have fascinated great minds, inspired great
deeds and aroused great hopes ever since.

THE AMAZING JESUS

I am far within the mark when I say that all the armies that ever marched, and all the navies that ever sailed, and all the parliaments that ever sat, and all the kings that ever reigned, put together, have not affected the life of humanity upon earth as has that one solitary life.

Today one third of the world's population professes to follow Jesus Christ—more than double the number of followers of any of the other great religions. And in the West we date our calendar from the estimated year of his birth.

What was Jesus really like?

Many people and movements have claimed him as their hero. Peering down the well of history, they have been delighted to see their own reflection! Revolutionaries see in him a fellow freedom fighter. Travellers see him as one of them.

In fact we modernize Jesus of Nazareth at our own peril. It is impossible to identify him simply as guru, guerrilla, or even (as the musical *Godspell* would have it) clown.

However, the tremendous variety of images testifies to one thing: the remarkable attraction and relevance of the carpenter from Galilee.

A person like us

What did the first disciples see in Jesus, as they walked the dusty roads with him, and visited the little towns of Galilee?

They saw a person like themselves. One who ate and slept, and sweated and wept. Whose feet got dirty and whose muscles ached.

But in other ways Jesus was quite extraordinary. Though not what we would call 'religious', he had a private life of prayer which was vital and mystifying. He called God 'Father', and urged his friends to do the same.

His stories, which were many, had an explosive quality. They somehow detonated in the mind, blowing out a lot of prejudice, and letting in a lot of light! Ordinary people with no special education found his teaching riveting.

Peace

And there were the miracles. In a quiet, almost self-effacing way, Jesus helped and healed dozens of disabled people. The blind and the lame, the deaf and dumb—even the disgusting and untouchable lepers—were restored to health, strength and independence. On a few occasions, he even brought the dead back to life.

Above all, Jesus was his own person—and this in an exciting way. He had a hard-won inner peace. A peace which he could share with others. A peace which was grounded in his complete trust in God his Father. Early in the morning, or late at night, or in the

'I am the way,' said Jesus. 'No one comes to the Father except by me.' If we aim to know God, Jesus opens the door and lights the way to knowing him.

high heat of the day, Jesus would pause for prayer. The result was that, however much he was hassled or interrupted, he never lost sight of who he was, or what he had to do.

And yet, it had to be admitted that there was a most embarrassing side to Jesus. For one thing, he kept company with the dregs of society. He liked nothing better than to dine with known cheats and thieves, and once allowed a prostitute to caress his feet—without even blushing.

He could also be extremely rude. He accused some very distinguished people of play-acting their beliefs and exploiting their status. In fact he told them in no uncertain terms that they stank!

Small wonder the common people heard him gladly.

THE GOSPELS

The story of Jesus is told in four Gospels: Matthew, Mark, Luke and John. They miss out some of the things we would most like to know, such as details of Jesus' appearance —his height, or the colour of his eyes.

Nevertheless, the Gospels provide dozens of episodes showing us how Jesus treated people. We see how he coped with popularity, handled critics, and taught disciples. We witness one interruption after another, as the poor and needy clamour for his help. We trace his steps to Jerusalem, where betrayal, injustice, and crucifixion awaited him.

All the time we hear questions:

- **'Who is he?'**

- **'What right has he?'**

- **'Where does he get it from?'**

On one occasion, Jesus asked his disciples for feedback from public opinion: 'Who do people say that I am?'

They told him that people were undecided. Everyone agreed that Jesus was a man of God; a prophet like Elijah. Some thought he might even be John the Baptist, back from the dead. But when Jesus pressed his friends for their personal opinion, Peter had no hesitation in blurting out, 'You are *the Christ.*'

JESUS AS HE WAS

How close can we get to Jesus?

Surely he comes from another world—northern Palestine, two thousand years ago. He never drove

Who did Jesus think he was?

We know from the accounts of his baptism and temptations that Jesus knew he was none other than God's Son. He had been sent by God on a rescue mission to save mankind from sin and death—a mission which was to cost him his life.

Jesus often called himself the 'Son of Man'. In Jewish scripture, the Son of Man was a divine person in a human form.

The Jewish hope was that he would come from God to establish an everlasting kingdom, bringing all people under God's kingly rule. And this was the title Jesus took to express his calling.

But time and time again Jesus warned his disciples, 'The Son of Man must *suffer.*' And so he did. Utterly alone, rejected, and nailed to a

wooden cross, Jesus finally brought earth and heaven together. It was through his death that he achieved what his teaching and miracles could never do: he opened a way back to God for lost humanity.

a car or caught a bus; never changed a fuse, made a phone call, or spent an evening watching television.

The Gospels show us Jesus as he *was*, and not as we would like him to be. He was a Jew. As a child he learned the Jewish law, sitting in the village synagogue-school, reciting it as we would recite nursery rhymes. From his early years, he worked with his father at the carpenter's bench. He knew what it was to get sawdust in his eye, and to patiently fit a yoke to the shoulders of an ox. He was a craftsman.

And the whole atmosphere and pace of his life was so different from ours—the heat of noon, the bleat of sheep, the silence of Sabbath...

What was it like to live in that world where only men counted in the synagogue, where women and children were considered relatively unimportant, and where scribes did your reading and writing for you? What was it like to hate Samaritans and to shake the dust of their country from your clothes? What was it like to be commandeered by a Roman soldier to carry his pack for a mile, or to cross the road to avoid a leper?

This was the world of Jesus. The world in which he worked and worshipped, laughed and cried. And yet he wasn't just the product of his environment.

Take, for example, his attitude to children. He saw something in them which everyone else was missing; a simplicity and trust which God would love to see in adults. Jesus not only observed this for himself, but taught it and lived it out against the grain of public opinion.

He thought for himself. He saw the stupidity of worrying about

The straightforward faith and trust of a child was held by Jesus to be a model for all who followed him.

Did Jesus really happen?

Did the friends and followers of Jesus tell the truth? Did the early writers tell the story the way it was, or did they let their imaginations run away with them?

- Was Jesus the son of a virgin?

- Did he really defeat death and return from the grave?

- Did he turn water to wine at a wedding, feed a multitude from a few loaves and fishes, walk on water, and still a storm?

Did Jesus really happen? His disciples assure us he did.

John, perhaps the closest of them all, who lived to a ripe old age in Ephesus, wrote this: 'We write to you about the Word of life, which has existed from the very beginning. We have heard it, and we have seen it with our eyes; yes, we have seen it, and our hands have touched it. When this life became visible, we saw it . . .'

John and the other disciples were quite convinced that they had seen something take place in their lifetime, before their very eyes, which had opened a whole new relationship between God and people.

In the New Testament we have 'flavour-sealed' accounts of Jesus, written by those eye-witnesses, or by those who knew the eye-witnesses.

The apostle Paul wrote his letters within living memory of the death and resurrection of Jesus. There were still many people around who could remember those events as readily as some today can remember the Second World War.

Jesus had been the most talked-about Jew of his day. When he arrived in Jerusalem that fateful Passover, the whole city had been alive with speculation as to what would happen. When he was furtively arrested under cover of darkness, rushed through the courts in the early hours of the morning and dreadfully executed, the entire population was aware of the event. It took place in the full glare of publicity. There were thousands of people who could say, 'It happened. I was there.'

More than that, the Gospels contain the memories of those who were touched most closely of all—Jesus' family and friends. When these people claimed they had seen Jesus gloriously alive after his death, were they telling the truth? Or were they in fact a team of liars and forgers? As the years went by, many gave their lives, suffering imprisonment and death for the cause. Would they have done so if they had known it was all a hoax? Surely the source of their gladness and courage was that the good news of Jesus was true.

How else can we explain the explosive growth of the church, from a handful of followers? At first they were outnumbered in Judaism alone by 30,000 to 1, yet they had such a quality of life and love and joy that the size of the group quickly multiplied. Before long we hear of the zealous Saul of Tarsus dramatically converted to the Christian faith. He was stopped in his tracks by the reality of the risen Christ. Soon he is dismissing his impeccable Jewish pedigree and qualifications as so much rubbish, compared with the supreme joy of 'knowing Christ'!

All in all, the impact of Jesus is astonishing. He spent only three years in the public eye. Three years in a fairly remote corner of the Roman Empire. He died in his early thirties—half the age of Karl Marx or Chairman Mao, to say nothing of Confucius, Buddha and Muhammad. Yet his life has changed the history of the world, and today 1400 million people worship him as God.

If there were no such person as Jesus, where did his teaching come from? Which brilliant and original mind coined those memorable phrases: 'do not cast pearls before swine', 'take the plank out of your own eye', 'render to Caesar', 'suffer the children to come unto me...'?

And the finest stories the world has ever heard—the Prodigal Son, the Good Samaritan, the Great Supper, and dozens of others—were they written, compiled and distributed by an unknown genius? The apostle Paul, for example, had one of the finest minds the world has ever seen; but he was one for long and tortuous sentences—pithy stories were hardly his speciality!

There is no doubt that in the Gospels we have a collection of sayings and stories which are very distinctive in manner, style and content.

They show us the mind of a single, unique teacher. His name is Jesus.

In the 2,000 years since the death and resurrection of Jesus, Christianity has grown and spread against all the odds to become a world faith.

Like layers of grime being cleaned from an old painting, scholars try to get to the original picture of Jesus' life and teaching.

money: 'How hard it is for a rich person to enter the kingdom of God.' A daring thing to say in a society that took wealth as a sign of God's blessing!

He saw through the finicky food laws—the endless debate about what was clean and unclean: 'There is nothing that goes into a person from the outside which can make them ritually unclean.' In other words, food can't make you wicked —it goes straight through you. The wickedness is already there.

In these and many other sayings, Jesus distilled truth into words. Of course, the things he said have been passed down many centuries and across many cultures. They have been translated into the languages of the world. All this has taken them a long way from the mouth of Jesus, who spoke Aramaic with the north-country accent of Galilee. The work of scholars has been to scrape away the grime of the years, so that we can see afresh the words of Jesus in something of their original colour.

When this is done, we come face to face with the amazing Jesus. We catch the impact and urgency of his mission. The kingdom of God is breaking in on us. The final judgment of the world is near. We see the pettiness of so many of our preoccupations: money, fashion, security and success. We begin to see things the Jesus way.

There are surprises. The parable of the Good Samaritan isn't about doing a good turn every day. The story of the Prodigal Son isn't about juvenile delinquency.

And there is fun. Jesus seems to have found camels as amusing as we do. He gives his disciples nicknames: James and John are the 'MacThunders', and unstable Simon is 'the Rock'. Jesus' laughter must have shattered many a Sabbath stillness—much to the annoyance of the pious neighbours.

Yes, Jesus *is* from another world. A first-century Jew steeped in the life and language of the Palestine of his day. But when we realize what he was saying and doing there and then, we are well on the way to hearing and understanding him for ourselves here and now—today.

Tracking the truth

A fragment of papyrus has been discovered dating from AD130. It is a piece from the jigsaw of John's Gospel, and it gives us a glimpse of Jesus on trial before Pilate, the Roman Governor. It includes an explicit statement by Jesus concerning his mission in life, as well as a mention of his death.

Pilate said to them, 'Then you yourselves take him and try him according to your law.' They replied, 'We are not allowed to put anyone to death.' (This happened in order to make the words of Jesus come true, the words he used when he indicated the kind of death he would die.) Pilate went back into the palace and called Jesus. 'Are you the King of the Jews?' he asked him.

And later the fragment continues:

So Pilate asked him, 'Are you a king, then?' Jesus answered, 'You say that I am a king. I was born and came into the world for this one purpose, to speak about the truth. Whoever belongs to the truth listens to me.'

It is very hard to account for this fragment if Jesus never existed!

Some people believe that there was such a person as Jesus, and that he was a remarkable man in many ways, but that his followers tended to exaggerate. The difficulty with this view is that even Jesus' enemies agreed that he performed miracles. In the Gospels, the teaching of Jesus and the miracles of Jesus go hand in hand. We can't have one without the

other, however convenient it would be to keep the Sermon on the Mount and discard the stilling of the storm.

Those who say that the facts about Jesus were blown up out of all proportion at a much later date must reckon with the letters of Paul. They are the earliest documents of Christianity, and they contain, full-fledged, the highest possible view of Jesus as the perfect image of God, and the key figure in time and eternity.

THE THINGS JESUS DID

It was not until Jesus was about thirty that he began his brief ministry; two or three years spent training disciples, preaching, and healing.

Jesus' life was all of a piece.

He did not merely talk about the love and power of the kingdom of God. He showed it. He lived it. He was the kingdom of God in person.

He broke all the rules of social etiquette. He dined with devious and dishonest tax collectors. He was seen in broad daylight talking to a woman who was known for her succession of lovers. He stopped an important conversation to welcome children and give them a hug. He touched lepers—and corpses.

When challenged about the company he kept, Jesus said, 'Healthy people don't need a doctor; sick people do.' He was attracted to those who were ill in mind or body because they were the very people he had come to help. He wanted them to be the first to enjoy the healing and peace of God's kingdom.

Jesus chose twelve men to share his life. These were his disciples, and they were a mixed bunch. They differed from one another in temperament, background and politics. But at the call of Jesus they were prepared to leave home, family and livelihood. At first they listened to his teaching and watched him at work. Later they were to go out in pairs to preach the

Jesus once said, 'I am among you as one who serves.' He was quick to see people's deepest needs and had the power and the love to meet them. In fact, the deeper people's needs, the more strongly Jesus was drawn to them.

good news of the kingdom themselves, and to show God's power in healing and exorcism.

It speaks volumes that Jesus not only united such diverse characters into a team, but that he also allowed them to subject him to the closest scrutiny day in and day out for something like three years.

Miracles happened!

There is no doubt at all that Jesus performed miracles of healing. Even his enemies agreed that he did so, and accused him of sorcery! In fact it is impossible to 'modernize' the story of Jesus by keeping his teaching and throwing away his miracles. The two go together so closely that you cannot have one without the other.

The miracles were a glimpse of the power of God.

Jesus healed all kinds of illness

The blind and deaf, the paralyzed and the diseased. People with leprosy, dropsy, haemorrhage, and fever—all were restored to health. On three occasions Jesus even raised the dead to life.

Unlike other wonder-workers, he effected the cures without elaborate ritual or mumbo-jumbo. He would perhaps touch the person he was healing, or take them by the hand. Once he mixed a muddy paste to put on a blind man's eyes. But Jesus was never sensational. He often told the person concerned not to go shouting about what had happened.

Jesus was an exorcist of evil spirits

Confronted by cases of demon-possession, he simply spoke with life-giving authority: 'Be healed', or 'Come out of him!' An army officer recognized that Jesus had the same kind of command over disease and demons as he had over his soldiers.

A handful of miracles were

Jesus was not 'religious'

Although Jesus got on very well with immoral outcasts, he was in constant friction with those who were religious. Religious people can find their security in rules and regulations (which they keep 'religiously'), which tend to squeeze God out.

The scribes and Pharisees were scrupulous in their religious observance. But, as Mark Twain has observed, 'They were good in the worst sense of the word'! They meticulously gave 10 per cent of their herbs to God, but ignored the greater issues of justice and mercy.

Jesus accused them of 'straining at gnats and swallowing camels'! And in his parable of the Pharisee and the tax collector, he showed that the Pharisee, despite his prize-winning prayer, was merely worshipping himself. It was the tax collector, the religious non-starter, whom God heard and forgave.

rather like magic. On one occasion, at a wedding, Jesus turned a large quantity of water into a very fine wine—which made a point.

Again, when a large crowd of people overstayed their time listening to him, Jesus fed them all from a few loaves and fishes.

And Lake Galilee was the setting for some extraordinary events: two record-breaking catches of fish, the stilling of a storm, and the sight of Jesus himself walking on water!

Miracles cannot happen!

There have been many attempts to explain away these events. Perhaps a single youngster reaching for his picnic reminded the rest of the crowd it was lunch-time—and they got out their sandwiches as well? Maybe Jairus' daughter was merely in a coma? Possibly the storm on Lake Galilee did just happen to stop at the moment Jesus spoke, but was it really a coincidence?

Before we make the Gospels a happy hunting-ground for our own pet theories, we have to answer a basic question.

If Jesus was really the Son of God, and the effects of God's power were to be seen when he was around, would such things as the miracles be possible?

It's a big 'if', but the answer is 'yes'. Unless the story of Jesus is all fiction, he clearly did things which cut across the 'laws of nature'.

But without the miracles, the story of Jesus would make very little sense, and be hardly worth the telling.

In all this, three things are worth bearing in mind.

- **It is unscientific to say 'the miracles could not have happened'.**

The scientific approach is surely to weigh the evidence and acknowledge the extraordinary circumstances. 'Laws of nature' are no more than 'what usually happens'.

- **In John's Gospel, the miracles are treated as 'signs'.**

When he cured blindness, the action was all of a piece with Jesus' description of himself as 'the Light of the World', and the application that he is the one who gives spiritual light. Again, the feeding of the crowd was far more than the happy sharing of a small boy's lunch. It was a sign that Jesus is 'the Bread of Life', and the food he gives to people's souls.

- **Jesus could not perform wonders where there was no faith.**

Faith in God was always the active ingredient in the healings of Jesus. He told a woman who had squeezed through the crowd to touch his cloak, 'Your faith has made you well.' Many of the healing stories emphasize the faith either of the patient or of those who asked for the cure on the patient's behalf. But where there was no faith, healing was impossible and Jesus was powerless to help.

A turn-up for the book

Jesus turned the values of his day upside-down. Those who count for nothing in this world are highly prized by God. In these sayings, known as 'The Beatitudes', Jesus describes their reward. Matthew has Jesus delivering these words on a hill—rather implying that they are the greatest thing since the giving of the Law on Mount Sinai!

Happy are those who
    know they are
    spiritually poor;
    the kingdom of heaven
        belongs to them!
Happy are those who
    mourn;
    God will comfort
        them!
Happy are those who
    are humble;
    they will receive
        what God has
        promised!
Happy are those
    whose greatest
    desire is to do
    what God
    requires;
    God will satisfy
        them fully!
Happy are those
    who are
    merciful to
    others;
    God will be
        merciful to them!

Happy are the pure in
    heart;
    they will see God!
Happy are those who
    work for peace;
    God will call them his
        children!
Happy are those who are
    persecuted because
    they do what God
    requires;

the kingdom of heaven
    belongs to them!

THE THINGS JESUS SAID

The first time Jesus preached, he was nearly lynched!

He was speaking in his home synagogue, to the people he had known since boyhood. Luke tells us that he read them a passage from the prophecy of Isaiah:

The Spirit of the Lord is upon me, because he has chosen me to bring good news to the poor.

He has sent me to proclaim liberty to the captives and recovery of sight to the blind; to set free the oppressed and announce that the time has come when the Lord will save his people.

He then rolled up the scroll, gave it back to the attendant, and sat down. His next words must have dropped like a bombshell. 'This passage of Scripture has come true today, as you heard it being read.' In other words, 'God is doing these things here and now. He is doing them through me!'

When Jesus sensed their scepticism and hostility, he quietly observed that it would be the same for him as it had been for Elijah and

---

Speaking the truth

Jesus was brilliant at speaking truth to a situation.

When a group of lawyers caught a woman committing adultery, they challenged him to sentence her to death as prescribed in the Law of Moses. After all, if he pardoned her, he was condoning her immorality.

But Jesus found a third way. He challenged any-one who was innocent to commence the stoning, and the group disappeared. Instead of condemning her to death, Jesus set her free. But he did not condone her actions. On the contrary, he commanded her not to sin again.

Asked about taxation, Jesus again cut through a complex issue with masterly simplicity. Was it right for Jews to pay taxes to Rome? If he approved, he was no friend of God's. If he disapproved, he was no friend of Caesar's.

Jesus asked for a Roman coin. 'Whose image and inscription is this?' he asked. 'Caesar's,' they replied. 'Then give to Caesar the taxes due to him, and give to God the things that are God's,' said Jesus.

He had refused to be trapped. But by observing that the money bore Caesar's image, he reminded them that people are made in the image of God. And were they giving God his due?

Elisha. Both those great prophets of the past had been rejected by their own people.

Within minutes the congregation had hauled him from the synagogue, dragged him to the edge of a precipice, and fully intended to kill him. But such was his authority that he was able to simply walk through the middle of the crowd and go on his way.

The whole episode was typical of the directness of his teaching and the division he was to cause.

Jesus talked constantly about the kingdom of God

For him, the kingdom was no pipe dream. It was already happening. He has not just lecturing on the theory; he was enjoying the practical!

At the heart of the kingdom was God's love.

God was searching for his people, like a shepherd going after a lost sheep. When even a single stray was found and brought home, the whole community was invited to rejoice. And there was gladness in heaven when a single miserable sinner was rescued and restored.

Jesus described God's search as like that of a woman who lost a coin from her dowry. She would not rest until she had painstakingly swept her dark house, and found it in her dustpan. Again, her success would result in a celebration with the neighbours.

Or God's love was like that of a father whose son had run away and squandered a fortune. Yet every day he kept a constant look-out until at last he saw his boy in the distance. Then, without standing on ceremony, he tucked up his robe and ran along the road to sweep the lad into his arms. And this (you will have guessed) was followed by a party!

The kingdom prayer

Jesus heralded a spiritual revolution when he dared to call God 'Abba', which means 'dear Father'.

The name of God was too holy to be defiled by human lips, and in the Essene manuscripts (found in the caves of Qumran in 1947) the name of God is too holy even to be written. Four dots replace the word.

Jesus, however, taught his disciples to approach God with the simple trust of a child with a father:

Our Father in heaven:
May your holy name be honoured;
may your kingdom come;
may your will be done on earth as it is
* in heaven.*
Give us today the food we need.
Forgive us the wrongs we have
* done, as we forgive the wrongs*
* that others have done to us.*
Do not bring us to hard testing,
but keep us safe from the Evil One.
THE GOSPEL OF MATTHEW

The lifestyle of the kingdom is trust in God:

I tell you not to worry about the food you need to stay alive or about the clothes you need for your body. Life is much more important than food, and the body much more important than clothes. Look at the crows: they don't sow seeds or gather a harvest; they don't have store-rooms or barns; God feeds them!

You are worth so much more than birds! Can any of you live a bit longer by worrying about it?

Look how the wild flowers grow: they don't work or make clothes for themselves. But I tell you that not even King Solomon with all his wealth had clothes as beautiful as one of these flowers. It is God who clothes the wild grass—grass that is here today and gone tomorrow, burnt up in the oven. Won't he be all the more sure to clothe you? How little faith you have!

But the coming of God's kingdom involved judgment as well.

It was like harvest time, when the crop is taken in. The wheat is stored, but the weeds are destroyed. There will be a home-coming for God's people, but a day of reckoning for his enemies.

It was like fishermen sorting their catch, or a shepherd separating sheep from goats.

Jesus used the everyday images and episodes of his time to help to get his message across.

28

It was like a master returning after a long absence and asking his servants how they had managed his property.

Jesus spoke simply. He took the images and episodes of every day and made windows into heaven. When pressed for a ruling on whom you should love (and whom you could therefore hate), Jesus told the story of a wounded traveller who was left for dead by two devout Jews, but rescued and most generously helped by a hated Samaritan. Anyone can love their friends, but the citizens of the kingdom love their enemies as well.

Confronted by greed, Jesus told the story of a very successful farmer who was planning his retirement. He was very wisely deciding to take things more easily, when he died suddenly in his sleep. By human standards he was very rich, but in God's sight he was an impoverished fool.

The kingdom of God is sure to win!

Some of Jesus' stories captured the irrepressible life of the kingdom. It might not seem a very promising start—a carpenter rabbi with a handful of followers—but God's victory was absolutely certain.

It was like a tiny mustard seed, scarcely visible to the naked eye, which would grow to be a mighty tree—a landmark and a shelter.

It was like a small amount of yeast in a large barrel of flour. It would quietly get to work until the whole quantity was leavened.

It was like a sower who, despite losing a lot of his precious seed to birds, thistles and drought, would reap a sensational harvest in the end.

JESUS CLAIMED TO BE GOD

The people who heard Jesus were openly astonished at his authority and confidence.

His teaching was peppered with 'It has been said in the past ... but *I* say ...', and his frequent 'I tell you' (or 'Take my word for it') was an unmistakable mark of his style.

Not only did he have a very sure touch in handling difficult questions, but he was willing to pit his judgment against time-honoured tradition. He even took issue with the Law of Moses when it came to the question of divorce.

Gradually it became clear, to friend and foe alike, that he was claiming God's authority to a very special degree.

He spoke of himself in a way which included one of the Old Testament names of God, 'I AM':

I am the bread of life. He who comes to me will never be hungry ... I am the light of the world. Whoever follows me will have the light of life and will never walk in darkness.

And most sensationally of all:

Before Abraham was born, I AM.

This was a claim to divinity which was so outrageous that he had to hide in the temple to avoid being stoned on the spot.

Jesus claimed the power and authority of God in other ways. He said he could forgive sins, that he would come in the clouds of heaven, sitting at the right hand of power, and that he could raise the dead.

And to the disciples he said quite simply: 'The Father and I are one.'

GOD TO THE RESCUE

The story of Jesus is the story of a rescue operation.

Almighty God set out to rescue his creation from futility and death, beginning with humanity. He did it by sending his Son, Jesus. The very name was a declaration of intent, for Jesus means 'God to the rescue'.

So it is that when Mark begins his Gospel, he gives us the happy ending right at the beginning. Despite the fact that a third of his account will be taken up with the depressing facts of Jesus' suffering and death, he is able to say without a shadow of doubt: 'This is the good news about Jesus Christ, the Son of God.'

The first Christians preached that God succeeded in his all-or-nothing rescue mission. And every episode of Jesus' life, from borrowed cradle to empty tomb, is narrated in the light of that victory.

When Jesus was born, angels sang out that God was seeking to make peace with humans. Christ's coming was a declaration of war on the kingdom of Satan, not on the human race. For humankind, his coming was a sign of God's overwhelming love, and his irrepressible desire to save. 'God loved the world so much,' says John in his Gospel, 'that he gave his only Son, so that everyone who believes in him may not die but have eternal life.'

All the Gospels speak of the conquest of sin and death through the dying and rising of Jesus. Even so, it was only after the resurrection that it dawned on the disciples what God had been doing all along. At every stage God had been present and active in Jesus. It had all taken

It's easy for us to understand the sense of relief and gratitude this climber must feel as he is rescued. Christians believe that God, through Jesus, has rescued his creation from futility and death. When we fully appreciate this, it's natural to want to thank and praise God.

place 'before their very eyes'! But only after the resurrection could they see it.

Through Jesus, God had been doing for humanity what they can never do for themselves. He had made a way by which self-centred, proud, disobedient people could be forgiven. It was a way of restoring that friendship with our Maker for which we have been made. And all this not through turning over a new leaf, or trying to be good, but by trusting that Jesus had rescued them.

Every other religion in the world is a DIY job. 'Do it yourself.' 'You can make it if you try.' The Christian faith is something completely different.

New life is God's free gift.

The supplier is Jesus Christ. Good News indeed!

3

THE HEART OF THE MATTER

The death of Jesus was inevitable. The Jewish leaders engineered it. The Roman soldiers carried it out. Somehow the hasty execution at Golgotha was at the very heart of God's plan. Jesus himself was born to die, and had repeatedly warned his disciples of the trauma that lay ahead.

THE INESCAPABLE CROSS

As an exciting and radical teacher, Jesus had threatened the whole structure of a legalistic religion. He had exposed the spiritual bankruptcy of the Jewish leaders, and aroused their jealousy.

As a dynamic and popular leader, he posed a threat to the political order—the Roman occupiers and their Jewish puppets. Again, his death was inevitable.

But most of all, the death of Jesus was unavoidable because God intended it. 'God so loved the world, that he gave his only Son . . .' Jesus himself said, calmly and emphatically, 'No one takes my life from me—I lay it down myself.'

The shadow

The cross of Christ has cast a shadow over the history of the world. That single event has made such a radical difference to so many people in so many places over so long a period, that it is quite impossible to imagine the human story without it.

Of course, if Jesus was really the Son of God, there must have been something very deep going on when he died. Again, it was horrible, and mystifying, that such a great and good person was exterminated like a common criminal. If the love of God was on show as never before, so was the depravity of humans.

But the first Christians said their own lives were completely changed by what Jesus did on the cross. Some said their sins had been forgiven through his death. Others said they had found peace of mind, peace with God.

So what had happened?

Jesus made a sacrifice

Sin separates us from God: it can lead only to death.

For centuries, Jews had killed animals. This was to show that the people had offended God's holiness deeply and deserved to die. What they did was symbolically to place their guilt on the head of an animal (preferably a prize specimen—the very best of the herd or flock) and then offer its life instead of their own.

The priest would take the animal's blood and pour it on the altar. This was the act of 'atonement'. It showed that the sin which led to death had been dealt with, and that God and the person or people concerned had been reconciled.

But for any thoughtful Jew, it was obvious that more was needed than the repeated slaughter of bullocks and sheep, costly and meaningful as that was. And it was John the Baptist who said, when he saw Jesus, 'There is the Lamb of God!' In other words, the death of Jesus (Son of God and perfect human) was the ultimate sacrifice for the waywardness and guilt of the whole human race.

Victory

The cross of Jesus marked the spot where a titanic battle was fought between the love of God and the forces of evil.

Right at the beginning of his ministry, when he was tempted by the devil, Jesus had given Satan notice to quit. By word and deed he had set about releasing men and women from the kingdom of darkness. His whole life had been a sustained onslaught on suffering, sin and death.

On the cross, the world, the flesh and the devil did their worst, and Jesus was apparently defeated.

But God raised his Son from death! The love and justice of God (his love for the world but his hatred of sin), had been completely satisfied and reconciled by the perfect sacrifice of Jesus.

From the death of Jesus onwards, sins can be forgiven and death defeated. The war between good and evil goes on, but the decisive battle has been won.

Jesus paid a ransom

Jesus' own explanation of his death was that he was giving himself as a ransom payment. For us a ransom is the money demanded by kidnappers or terrorist groups as the condition on which they release a prisoner. In Roman times, a ransom was the price paid to secure the freedom of a slave. In fact the slave and the person who was to pay his ransom would take part in a religious ceremony at which the money was paid to the slave's owner in the presence of a pagan god: the idea being that the slave then belonged to the god, and so was a free man.

Jesus took this idea and developed it to show the meaning of his death. His life was a payment to secure the freedom of men and women from the slavery of sin and death. The result was that people had a new owner. They now belonged to God, whose service is perfect freedom.

Jesus went through hell

The most painful problem of life is the existence of suffering—especially when that suffering is undeserved. If God is loving, and his creation is good, why is there so much heartbreak and misery?

There is no simple answer. Illness, injustice, disease and death are facts of life in a world spoiled by sin and hostile to God.

Why doesn't God *do* something about it, we cry.

He did.

When Jesus came to this world, he did not excuse himself from suffering. Indeed, on the cross he plumbed the very depths of degradation and despair.

In later years, Peter saw the death of Jesus as an example of how to face and endure injustice: 'When he was insulted, he did not answer back ... When he suffered, he did not threaten, but placed his hopes in God, the righteous Judge.'

Jesus took what was coming to us

As Jesus died, he shouted at the top of his voice, 'It is finished!'

'Finished' was the word Greeks wrote across bills that had been paid. On the cross Jesus took our account, our eternal deficit with God, and met it in full.

He suffered the disaster and death that should by rights have been ours, and we can never even begin to know what that cost him. He went through an experience which we thoroughly deserve but would be unable to bear and could never survive. Peter again: 'Christ himself carried our sins in his body to the cross, so that we might die to sin and live for righteousness. It is by his wounds that you have been healed.'

THE EASTER FAITH

Jesus' body was put in a rock tomb on the Friday of Passover weekend. By Sunday it had vanished. It was a shock for which the disciples were totally unprepared. The Jewish authorities bribed the soldiers who had been guarding the tomb to say

A hole in history

Quite apart from the evidence of the Gospel, there are the facts of history to reckon with.

The worldwide movement we know as the Christian Church can be traced back in history to Palestine in the year AD30 or thereabouts.

Something happened after the death of Jesus which changed his followers from cowards to heroes. Within a few years they had taken the Good News from Jerusalem through Asia Minor to Rome itself. Would they have carried the message of resurrection so convincingly if they had known it was all a lie? And would so many have undergone martyrdom, as indeed they did, if they were all along harbouring the secret that Jesus was in fact dead?

And what made the early Christians change their day of worship from Sabbath (Saturday) to Sunday? Surely it was the central fact of the Easter faith, that Christ was raised from death on a Sunday morning?

Millions of people down the ages have experienced the presence and power of the risen Christ. They would all echo the words of Sir Malcolm Sargent: 'Without Christ I cannot live; with him I cannot die.'

Something sensational happened that first Easter morning which left a hole in history. A hole the size and shape of the resurrection of Jesus.

that they had fallen asleep, and that some followers of Jesus had seized the corpse.

• Did the disciples steal the body?

The accounts in the Gospels show us a demoralized and frightened group of people. The tomb was guarded. They certainly had no leader capable of planning and carrying out a raid on the tomb.

• Did the authorities, Jewish or Roman, intervene?

For the Roman Governor, the unsavoury episode was already closed. But if the priests had managed to persuade him to change the burial place, surely they would have silenced the disciples by producing the remains? The fact that neither side knew the whereabouts of the body is a most exciting and significant aspect of the evidence.

Jesus began to appear to his disciples

Mary of Magdala was the first to see him. According to John's Gospel, she was weeping at the empty tomb, deeply grieving the death of her master, and angry and frustrated that his body had not been allowed to rest in peace. When the risen Jesus appeared to her, the writer tells us with disarming

The resurrection of Jesus declares God's principle of life in death.

frankness that, through her tears, she thought she saw the gardener! Anyone forging a legend would hardly include such a detail, and would probably not choose a reformed prostitute as the first witness.

Later the same day, Jesus joined two of the disciples as they walked home to their village. This time Luke tells the story and again every observation rings true. They don't immediately recognize Jesus (though their hearts are strangely warmed when he explains scripture to them). But after they have invited him to their home and he breaks bread with them, it suddenly dawns on them who he is.

Ascension

Jesus appeared to his disciples many times after his resurrection. It was as though he was in a state of 'overlap' between earth and heaven. He was able to come and go, teaching his disciples, and assuring them beyond a shadow of doubt that he was alive again.

This went on for about six weeks. At the end of that time, Jesus told his disciples to wait in Jerusalem until they received the Holy Spirit. The Spirit would fill them with power, and enable them to spread the Good News not only in Jerusalem, but to the surrounding areas, and indeed to the ends of the earth.

Then Jesus was received into heaven, and they saw him no more.

Luke, a careful historian, describes what happened when Jesus parted from his disciples for the last time.

After saying this, Jesus was taken up to heaven as they watched him, and a cloud hid him from their sight.

They still had their eyes fixed on the sky as he went away, when two men dressed in white suddenly stood beside them and said, 'Galileans, why are you standing there looking up at the sky? This Jesus, who was taken from you into heaven, will come back in the same way that you saw him go to heaven.'

Jesus visibly left his disciples and the earth and returned to heaven. He was received back into his father's presence, and resumed the glory which is rightfully his.

Just as he was God's representative on earth, he is now humanity's representative in heaven. Heaven is where God is. It is 'higher' than earth, not in the sense of being 'above the bright blue sky', but in the sense of being a perfectly harmonious realm of the spirit.

Jesus, in passing into that realm, has secured free and confident access to the presence of God for all who follow him.

• Had Jesus merely 'revived'?

Perhaps Jesus had never really died, but only fainted from loss of blood? Maybe he felt better after lying in the cool tomb, and eventually managed to break out?

But this theory ignores the fact that the Romans had double-checked his death. A soldier had pierced Jesus' side, to ensure he was dead. And would a brutally beaten and crucified man recover sufficiently to roll the stone from the mouth of the tomb, overcome the guards, and walk miles on wounded feet? Even had he done so, Jesus would hardly have cut a dash as the Prince of Life!

• Were the disciples having hallucinations?

Everything we know of the resurrection indicates that it took the disciples entirely by surprise. The last person they expected to see was Jesus.

The risen Christ was seen by Mary Magdala, who had watched him die. But she was not the only witness. The risen Christ was seen by Matthew, the hard-headed tax collector, Peter the rugged fisherman, and Thomas the sceptic. On one occasion, five hundred people all claimed to have seen Jesus of Nazareth gloriously alive after his death on the cross.

Nor were these appearances all in the eerie light of dawn or suggestive twilight. They happened at all sorts of times and places, and to a wide variety of people.

Jesus had been raised from death

Gradually a profound conviction settled over the little group of disciples. Jesus had done more than survive crucifixion. He was no pale invalid slowly recuperating from a dreadful ordeal. He was gloriously alive!

Nor was he a vague ghost. He could be clearly seen and distinctly heard. He could be touched. He could eat. And yet he was the same Jesus who had been seen hanging on the cross. The marks of his suffering could still be seen and felt.

Somehow he was now the other side of death. God had raised his Son from the grave. And now Jesus had a resurrection body: a spiritual body, mysteriously different, but recognizably the same.

SO WHAT?

What does the resurrection mean for us today? It means Jesus was who he said he was.

Paul wrote his first letter to the Christians at Corinth in about AD55. In it he reminds his readers what he had told them round about AD49.

I passed on to you what I received, which is of the greatest importance: that Christ died for our sins, as written in the Scriptures; that he was buried and that he was raised to life three days later, as written in the Scriptures; that he appeared to Peter and then to all twelve apostles. Then he appeared to more than five hundred of his followers at once, most of whom are still alive, although some have died. Then he appeared to James, and afterwards to all the apostles.

Here we have the roots of the Christian faith: the Jesus facts carefully passed on by word of mouth from the eye-witnesses, the apostles. Paul had checked the story with them just a few years after the crucifixion and resurrection. He had found their evidence totally convincing, and knew of hundreds of other witnesses who were still alive to tell the tale. It was the resurrection which proved that Jesus was the Christ. Without it there would be no Jesus Christ and no Christianity.

Jesus had made a way back to God

When Jesus died, he shouted, 'It is finished!' A sacrifice had been provided for the guilt and aggro and spite of the human race. The death penalty had been paid in full. Jesus had taken on himself the sin which separates humankind from God

Putting it the other way, the apostle Paul writes bluntly: 'And if Christ has not been raised, then your faith is a delusion and you are still lost in your sins.' And he adds that if such is the case, 'we deserve more pity than anyone else in the world'!

The new life of Jesus is the guarantee of our own new life. Jesus was not raised from death so that he could enjoy eternity in splendid isolation. He said to his disciples, 'Because I live, you shall live too.' Paul calls Jesus 'the prototype'—the first of many. Jesus has bridged the gap between God and humankind, so that all who trust him can safely cross the gulf of death.

And resurrection starts now! Because Jesus is alive, we can enjoy his presence today. He is our contemporary Saviour and Lord. As Paul wrote in a rare burst of journalese, 'Person in Christ, New Creature!' For himself he could say with all his heart, 'It is no longer I who live, but Christ who lives in me.'

4

GOD'S OWN PEOPLE

The place was Jerusalem, and the occasion was the Jewish festival of Pentecost. The Christian faith burst on an unsuspecting world at nine o'clock on a Sunday morning, probably in the year AD30.

THE CHURCH HAS LIFT-OFF

Jesus had told the disciples to wait in Jerusalem for the coming of his Spirit. Suddenly, while they were in prayer, the promised gift was given.

Luke describes the coming of the Spirit as 'like a strong wind blowing', and 'like tongues of fire'. The believers were filled with an invisible, burning power, which was none other than the close presence of God.

And they began to speak in foreign languages! Pilgrims who had come from all over the known world were astonished to hear these peasants from Galilee praising God in the tongues and dialects of home. God was giving the spread of the gospel a flying start.

It was Peter who preached. With the support and consent of the other disciples, he made the ringing claim that Jesus had risen from the grave. And this is Jerusalem, within two months of the crucifixion, and within two miles of the tomb.

In accordance with his own plan God had already decided that Jesus would be handed over to you; and you killed him by letting sinful men crucify him. But God raised him from death!

That day the nucleus of one hundred and twenty believers was expanded by three thousand converts!

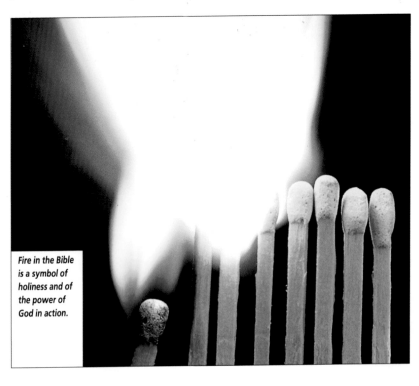

Fire in the Bible is a symbol of holiness and of the power of God in action.

THE JESUS PEOPLE

The early church was unstoppable.

It began with the preaching of the apostles in Jerusalem. When arrested and threatened with imprisonment and death, they argued their case with even greater vigour! Their message was that Jesus was the promised deliverer, the Messiah, and that all should turn to him for forgiveness and new life with God.

The good news was further commended by the remarkable warmth and genuineness of friendship among the believers. They shared their belongings, helped those in need, and met every day to worship in the temple or enjoy meals in one another's homes.

Things they said about Jesus

'The Christ', 'Messiah', 'God's Chosen One'—these were the titles given to Jesus by his followers.

After the resurrection, even doubting Thomas fell on his knees and declared in awe, 'My Lord and my God!' There in the upper room, Jesus accepted the kind of worship which Jews reserved for God alone.

It was not that Jesus had become the Son of God. The truth was that he had always existed, independent of time and space.

In John's Gospel, Jesus is called 'the Word'.

Before the world was created, the Word already existed; he was with God, and he was the same as God. The Word was active in the creation of the universe. The Word was the source of life. Taking up the same theme, Paul wrote that Jesus was 'the visible likeness of the invisible God'. The whole of God was present in Jesus, and it is through him that the creation hangs together. Without him there would be disintegration and chaos.

So what happened when God became a person? Was he merely pretending to be human? Paul explains in his letter to the Philippians.

He [Jesus] always had the nature of God, but he did not think that by force he should try to become equal with God. Instead of this, of his own free will he gave up all he had, and took the form of a servant. He became like man and appeared in human likeness. He was humble and walked the path of obedience all the way to death—his death on the cross. For this reason God raised him to the highest place above and gave him the name that is greater than any other name. And so, in honour of the name of Jesus all beings in heaven, on earth, and in the world below will fall on their knees, and all will openly proclaim that Jesus Christ is Lord, to the glory of God the Father.

There was a contagious gladness about the group, and their numbers quickly increased.

At first the membership was exclusively Jewish, but before long it became clear that the Christian butterfly was to leave its Hebrew cocoon. One after another, barriers and prejudices were broken down.

For example, the church in Jerusalem was shocked when Samaritans came to faith in Jesus. Two apostles, Peter and John, rushed over to see for themselves, welcomed them in Christ, and helped them receive the Holy Spirit.

An African was converted and baptized on his way home to Ethiopia. Saul of Tarsus, the church's cruellest persecutor, was dramatically converted on the Damascus road, and became the apostle Paul.

Paul

Paul was a small man with a bald head and bandy legs. At least, that's one description of him which has survived the centuries.

We know from his own writings that he had no great natural presence. He was an unimpressive speaker, and he suffered from what he called a 'thorn in the flesh'— which may have been a form of epilepsy.

Born Saul of Tarsus, he grew up in Turkey, which had long been part of the Greek world. His family were Jews, and his father had the status of a Roman citizen. A Roman citizen with a Greek mind and a Jewish heart, Paul was uniquely qualified to bridge the gap between Jews and Gentiles.

As a young man, Saul travelled to Jerusalem to train as a rabbi. There he was incensed by the followers of 'The Way'—a new heresy which claimed that Jesus of Nazareth was Messiah. Once qualified, he set about persecuting them with a will.

He was in full flight, heading for the believers in Damascus with threats of murder on his lips, when he had a blinding vision of the risen Christ. In the most famous turnabout of history, Saul of Tarsus was converted to Christianity. In due course he became Paul the apostle, perhaps the brightest jewel in the early church's crown.

It is impossible to over-estimate the part played by Paul in the spread of the Christian faith.

In the course of three epic journeys, he was imprisoned, whipped, stoned and shipwrecked. In city after city he contacted the little Jewish communities, and told them the good news of Jesus the Messiah. He himself counted his impeccable Jewish pedigree as 'so much rubbish' once he had breathed the freedom and love of Christ. If the folk in the synagogues rejected him, he would declare: 'My conscience is clear; now I shall go to the Gentiles.'

Starting from Antioch (where the nickname 'Christians' originated), Paul first took the gospel to Cyprus and Asia Minor, planting churches in a number of centres.

On his second journey, he consolidated the existing work, and then crossed over to Europe, where he worked in

Peter surprised himself and everyone else by going into the home of Cornelius, an officer in the occupying Roman army. It was a momentous event, taking the new faith not just to Jews or Jewish sympathizers, but to non-Jews, called 'Gentiles'.

Inevitably, the church in Jerusalem was persecuted. But this had the unexpected benefit that the believers were scattered over a wider area, and wherever they went they talked about Jesus. The gospel was 'gossiped' just as much as it was 'preached'.

Before long a fascinating church was established in the cosmopolitan city of Antioch. Second only to Rome, Antioch provided the ideal springboard into Asia Minor. From there Paul and his team of missionaries

Philippi and Athens. Flogged by Jews, imprisoned by Romans, and taunted by Greeks, he never gave up.

Finally, he was arrested while on a visit to Jerusalem. As a Roman citizen, he was entitled to appeal to Caesar and this he did. The voyage to Rome nearly ended in disaster when the ship was wrecked on the coast of Malta. When he finally arrived in Rome, he was placed under house arrest.

Paul is last heard of in the Bible awaiting trial in Rome. The story goes that he was eventually executed during the vicious persecution of Christians by the Emperor Nero.

Paul's letters, often written from prison, are the earliest writings in the New Testament. They give a vivid picture of Paul himself and the problems he faced.

We glimpse the early church, warts and all: pride, jealousy and backbiting at Corinth; tight-lipped and insensitive legalism among the churches of Galatia. And then there were the questions such as, if Christ made you free, were you free to be immoral? Did non-Jews who became Christians have to take on board the burden of the Jewish Law, including circumcision?

Time and time again we see Paul rescuing the infant Christian faith from Jewish attempts to strangle it with legalism, or Gentile attempts to suffocate it by shrouding it in mystery.

It was largely thanks to Paul that the gospel survived and began to break down racial, cultural and social barriers. In his letter to the Galatians Paul said:

There is no longer any distinction between Gentiles and Jews, circumcised and uncircumcised, barbarians, savages, slaves, and free men, but Christ is all, Christ is in all. You are the people of God; he loved you and chose you for his own.

pioneered Christianity throughout the Graeco-Roman world.

The group of believers was one in mind and heart. No one said that any of his belongings were his own, but they all shared with one another everything they had. With great power the apostles gave witness to the resurrection of the Lord Jesus, and God poured rich blessings on them all.

FROM THE ACTS OF THE APOSTLES

NEW LIFE—NEW LIFESTYLE

The early Christians had a quality of life and lifestyle which marked them out as followers of Jesus.

They had a 'one-anotherness' among themselves; a committed love which put Christ and others before self. They went beyond all known bounds of behaviour by forgiving their enemies and praying for those who so bitterly persecuted them.

They had an infectious joy and

Christian leadership

The church has organized itself in a variety of ways over the centuries. Jesus, of course, had trained and commissioned the apostles. Their prime responsibility was to be witnesses to the truth about Jesus. After all, they were the ones who had shared his life, seen his death, and met him alive after his resurrection.

But the apostles were joined by others: deacons who handled administration, prophets who spoke God's word with startling insight, and teachers who deepened people's

understanding of the faith.

When Paul wrote to the Christians at Ephesus, he listed the various departments of church leadership: 'apostles, prophets, evangelists, pastors and teachers'. In each case, these were functions for which people had been equipped by the Spirit of God. Spiritual gifts were always for the benefit of others, and never for personal prestige.

Another thought-provoking aspect of the New Testament church was the absence of any professional clergy! There was no need now

for sacrifices, so no need for a priesthood to represent people to God. Everyone was a priest! And every member of the Christian family had a part to play, a service to give, and gifts to contribute. The bad old days of overactive priests and passive congregations were still in the future!

Handing down the truth

Whenever Christians gather, they remember that on a certain night their Founder said and did certain things. On that same night he was arrested by his enemies and put on trial. The following day he was executed by crucifixion.

This memory, handed down from one generation to the next, can be traced back to Palestine in the years when Pontius Pilate was the Roman Governor. It may even be that the day of crucifixion, the first Good Friday, can be dated precisely as April AD30. And whenever the story of Jesus was told, it was noticeable that it was his death which was so significant. His parables had been brilliant and his miracles amazing, but they faded into insignificance when compared with the drama of the cross.

We glimpse the living chain of memory within the church in a letter written by a French bishop, Irenaeus, who died at Lyons about the year AD200. Writing to an old friend, Florinus, he recalls their student days in Asia Minor, when they attended the lectures of Bishop Polycarp. Polycarp (who had died in AD155 when was well into his eighties) used to tell them stories about 'John the disciple of the Lord' whom he had known personally many years before.

So when Irenaeus celebrated Communion with fellow-Christians in Lyons, he was passing on something he had been told by his old teacher, whose friend had been there when it happened!

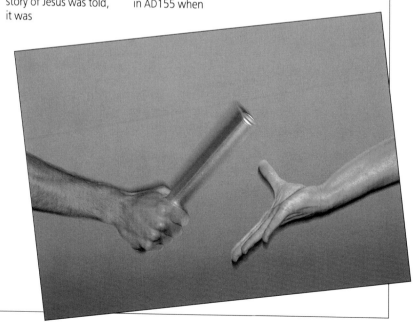

47

Signs of membership

Two simple ceremonies have always been part of the life of the church in every age and place. They are Baptism and Holy Communion.

● Baptism

A drenching in water which represents at best a wash and at worst a drowning! As a wash, it was a sign that the believer was turning to God for cleansing in the name of Christ, and making a new start in life. As a mini-drowning, it was a sign that the believer was dying to his or her old life and emerging again to the new life of Jesus.

It was a familiar sign to Jews, who circumcised male converts and baptized both men and women. They also counted children of believing parents as part of the family of faith until they were old enough to understand for themselves.

John the Baptist had caused a sensation by baptizing men and women who had been committed to Judaism all their lives. For John, baptism was a sign of 'repentance'—a change of mind about God, and a new readiness to serve him.

Jesus commanded his disciples to 'go to all peoples everywhere and make them my disciples: baptize them in the name of the Father, the Son and the Holy Spirit . . .' Ever since, water baptism has been the sign by which the Christian church has marked and welcomed those who have newly come to faith in Christ.

● Holy Communion

Also known as the Mass, the Eucharist and the Lord's Supper. A simple meal through which Christians remember the death and resurrection of Christ. On the night of his arrest, Jesus broke some bread and gave it to each of his disciples, with the words, 'This is my body, which is for you. Do this in memory of me.' At the end of the meal (which was probably a Passover celebration) Jesus took a cup of wine and said, 'This cup is God's new covenant, sealed with my blood. Whenever you drink it, do so in memory of me.'

So Christians have always shared in broken bread and poured out wine, just as they share in the fact that Jesus' body was broken on the cross and his blood shed for the sins of the world. This sharing, or 'fellowship', is both with the risen Jesus and with one another. It is a sharing of a common life, a new life made possible by the death and resurrection of Jesus.

Both Baptism and Communion are known as 'sacraments'— visible reminders of God at work. Just as a wedding ring is far more than a band of gold (it represents a married life of unending love); so Baptism and Communion are more than a wash and a meal. They mark the beginning and the continuation of the Christian life.

praise, and displayed a simple trust in God and peace of mind even when they were under attack. Not many of them were wealthy, yet they showed an unfailing generosity to the poor and needy. Not many were clever, yet they lived by standards of honesty and truth which shook the pagan world in which they lived, and gave an authentic ring to their message.

Such was the quality of their love that a new Greek word had to be found to describe it. That word was *agape*, selfless love. The world had never seen anything like it. Agape was the hallmark of the Jesus Revolution, and all an outsider could say was, 'See how these Christians love one another!'

Of course the church was far from perfect. There were misunderstandings and mistakes, and no doubt the groups of believers had more than their share of frauds and fanatics. But in spite of everything, including persecution, the simple love and truth of this new society was to conquer the Roman Empire and win the world.

Jesus' life was one of service to others. To follow him is not some theoretical notion, but a matter of laying ourselves open to the needs of others.

Passover

Jewish Passover and Christian Communion are closely linked.

On the night of their deliverance from slavery in Egypt, each Israelite family killed a perfect lamb and daubed its blood on the outside door of the house. That night the Angel of Death swept through Egypt, and the eldest sons of the Egyptians died. But when the angel saw the blood on the doors of the Israelites' homes, he 'passed over' the household, and they escaped the judgment which was falling on the land.

The Passover meal became an annual event for Jewish families, and continues to this day.

When Jesus came, he saw himself in terms of the Passover lamb. It was his life, freely offered, which would be the complete sacrifice for sin, and the means by which a new exodus could take place. The first exodus had been from slavery in Egypt to freedom in the promised land. The new exodus would spring humankind from the prison of sin and death and provide a new life in the family of God.

5

READ ALL ABOUT IT

Christians believe that God has made himself known in various ways: in his creation, and more clearly still in the pages of the Bible. Here we build up a detailed picture of the mind, will and character of the living God; a picture we could never complete from the evidence of creation alone.

THE BIBLE

In creation

The wonders of creation are evidence that there has been a Maker at work. 'How clearly the sky reveals God's glory!' exclaims one of the Psalms; and Paul adds in his letter to the Christians at Rome: 'Ever since God created the world, his invisible qualities, both his eternal power and his divine nature, have been clearly seen; they are perceived in the things that God has made.'

In Scripture

The Bible reveals God at work in history, and particularly in his dealings with Israel, the 'chosen people'.

Messages of God's love and anger were delivered at point-blank range by Israel's prophets. Their characteristic phrase, 'the Lord says', sounds like a trumpet through the pages of the Old Testament.

The Old Testament is the first, and larger, section of the Bible. It is really a mini-library of thirty-nine books, including law, history, poetry, prophecy, and practical advice.

The New Testament contains twenty-seven books, including four different accounts of the life of Jesus (the Gospels), an account of the birth and growth of the church (the Acts of the Apostles), several letters (most of them written by Paul), and the Revelation of John.

While the Old Testament books were written by a number of authors over a period of about a thousand years, the New Testament books were all written within living

The Torah: God's life-line

The Jews' most precious possession was, and is, the Torah; the loving Law of God.

The Psalmist delighted in it, like a dog with a bone.

Even today, when a Jewish teacher comes to the end of the Books of the Law (the first five books of the Bible), he reads the opening words of Genesis, to show that he begins all over again.

The Law is God's own instruction on how to live in the world he has made. Obedience to the Law spells health and wealth, long life and good days.

Israel, remember this! The Lord—and the Lord alone—is our God. Love the Lord your God with all your heart, with all your soul, and with all your strength. Never forget these commands that I am giving you today. Teach them to your children. Repeat them when you are at home and when you are away, when you are resting and when you are working. Tie them on your arms and wear them on your foreheads as a reminder. Write them on the doorposts of your houses and on your gates.

THE BOOK OF DEUTERONOMY

memory of the death and resurrection of Jesus. In other words, they are all-important eye-witness, or first-generation, accounts of what happened.

THE GOD WHO MAKES PROMISES

The story of the Jewish nation began with a promise.

God promised a man called Abram that he would be the father of a great people, a nation, and that they would have a land of their own. God's plan was to so guide and bless Abram's descendants, that the world would be able to see the kind of God he is.

The promise God made to Abram was known as the 'covenant', and has always been the corner-stone of the Jewish experience. It was renewed with each successive generation. Abram was given a new name, Abraham. In his old age, he and his wife Sarah had a son, Isaac. Isaac had two sons, Esau and Jacob.

God's purpose frequently seemed to hang by a thread. Not only was Isaac born to a very elderly mother, but he was also nearly sacrificed as a child! Jacob, as the younger son, did not qualify to inherit God's promise to his father. In fact he obtained Isaac's blessing by pretending to be his brother Esau, and deceiving the old man who was sitting in a dark tent and was nearly blind anyway. Despite this rather shaky start, it was to Jacob that God gave the name Israel, and from him

that the Israelites traced their descent.

At first sight, God's promise was never fulfilled. Certainly Abraham didn't live to see it. On his death, he had only one true son (hardly a nation!), and a small burial ground (scarcely the promised land!).

The same was true for Isaac and Jacob. Although they pastured their flocks in Palestine, they in no way possessed it. By the standards of their day, they were rootless, powerless, and ignorant.

Had God forgotten his promises, or failed to keep his word?

Covenant

There are a number of covenants in the Old Testament, of which three are especially important.

● The covenant with Abraham

God promised to give Abraham the land of Canaan.

● The covenant with the Israelites

God promised them, through Moses, that they would be his Chosen People.

● The covenant with David

God promised him that he would always have descendants, and that his kingdom would last for ever.

A covenant was sometimes in the nature of a bargain. When God committed himself to the people of Israel, for example, he promised to look after them and protect them. They were his subjects, and he their Lord. At the same time, the people had to give their undivided loyalty to God, and keep his laws.

But when God made his covenants with Abraham and David, there were no conditions to be met by the men concerned. God had somehow set his heart on them to bless them—in much the same way as a person might determine to leave someone a fortune in his will. All the emphasis is on what God has decided to do.

The Lord said to Abram, 'Leave your native land, your relatives, and your father's home, and go to a country that I am going to show you. I will give you many descendants,

and they will become a great nation. I will bless you and make your name famous, so that you will be a blessing.

I will bless those who bless you, but I will curse those who curse you. And through you I will bless all the nations.'

When Abram was seventy-five years old, he started out from Haran, as the Lord had told him to do; and Lot went with him. Abram took his wife Sarai, his nephew Lot, and all the wealth and all the slaves they had acquired in Haran, and they started out for the land of Canaan.

THE BOOK OF GENESIS

54

The descendants of Israel trusted that he had done nothing of the sort. God was utterly faithful, and his promises would stand for all eternity. Therefore it was only a matter of time before the hopes raised in the hearts of their ancestors would be fulfilled.

THE STORY OF THE PEOPLE OF GOD

Some time around the year 1250BC, a rabble of Hebrew slaves escaped from the clutches of their Egyptian overlords.

Their leader was a man named Moses, an exiled prince of Egypt with Hebrew blood in his veins.

Moses

It was Moses' conviction that Yahweh, the Living God, was renewing his commitment to the children of Israel, the Hebrews. He was demanding their release from slavery.

Not surprisingly, the ruling Pharaoh, Ramesses II, was at first sceptical and then downright hostile. After all, he stood to lose the cheap labour which was building his treasure cities. Eventually he was obliged to give way because of a series of terrible plagues which were inflicted on the Egyptians by Moses' new-found God.

The last of these, and the one which finally changed Pharaoh's mind, was the sudden death of every firstborn son and animal in the land.

Passover

The night before they left Egypt, the Hebrews ate a final meal. They killed a lamb for every household and splashed its blood on the doorposts and lintels outside. This was a sign to God to 'pass over' the family and spare the firstborn son. They then roasted the lamb and ate it quickly, with unleavened bread—there was no time to let the dough rise before baking it. Even as they ate, they had their bags packed and were dressed for the journey. By dawn they were on their way.

Exodus

They had scarcely gone any distance when they came to a stretch of open water known as the Sea of Reeds. This would have been an impossible obstacle, had not God miraculously intervened. He caused a strong east wind to dry the marsh, and the entire company was able to cross in safety.

Meanwhile, Pharaoh had already changed his mind, and Egyptian chariots were in hot pursuit. As they swept across the reed beds, the strong wind slackened and the water began to return. The chariot wheels became bogged down in the mud, and both horses and men were drowned.

To this day, the Jews look back to the Exodus (which means 'way out') as the birth of their nation. It was the point at which they realized their identity as God's people. Yahweh, the Living God, rescued them from bondage and despair and, against all the odds, gave them a present freedom and a future hope.

The seal of freedom

In due course, the children of Israel were led to the slopes of Mount Sinai. Here God revealed himself in earthquake, fire and storm. He was awesome and unapproachable in his holiness. And yet he was on their side!

At Sinai, God bound himself to Israel in an everlasting covenant, and delivered to Moses his Law.

Strange as it may seem, the covenant of Sinai was not legalistic! It is true that at this point the Ten Commandments were given, but these were part of the privilege of belonging to God.

Israel did not earn freedom by keeping the Law. The Law was given *after* deliverance from Egypt. It was intended to set a seal on the people's freedom and enable them to live full lives.

The Ten Commandments

The first four commandments relate to God.

I am the Lord your God who brought you out of Egypt, where you were slaves. Worship no god but me.

God establishes his identity as the one who delivered his people from Egypt. He alone is worthy of their worship.

Do not make for yourselves images of anything in heaven or on earth or in the water under the earth...

People are not to make images or idols of God. He is all-powerful and invisible. Any manmade idol, however well-intentioned, would not only appear to reduce him, but would be dumb, powerless, and easily dismissed.

Do not use my name for evil purposes...

God is holy, and his name (which includes his reputation) is to be treated with the utmost reverence. It is not to be used as a swear word, or as a guarantee on empty promises.

Observe the Sabbath and keep it holy...

One day in the week is to be kept as the Sabbath. It is a holy day, dedicated to God. It is a time for worship and rest—a taste of heaven.

The last six commandments relate to other people.

Respect your father and your mother, so that you may live a long time in the land that I am giving you.

Parents and elders are to be respected. In this way family life will be strong, and the national life secure.

Do not commit murder.

Human life is sacred.

Do not commit adultery.

Marriage is an exclusive commitment between husband and wife, and must not be undermined by either partner having an affair.

Do not steal.

A secret of stable community is respect for the property of others. This applies both to personal possessions and personal reputations.

Do not accuse anyone falsely.

Speaking and living the truth is absolutely vital.

THE PROMISED LAND

After a generation of wandering around the wilderness of Sinai, the children of Israel conquered the land of Canaan, under the leadership of Joshua. For some years they were led by judges, of whom the most famous was the prophet Samuel. But as time went on, the people began to clamour for a king.

Samuel argued that God was the ruler of Israel, and that they didn't need a king like other nations. Eventually the pressure for a strong human leader was so great that God chose a tall, handsome and gifted young man, and Samuel anointed him. His name was Saul.

Do not desire another man's house; do not desire his life, his slaves, his cattle, his donkeys, or anything else that he owns.

Envy is the 'domino' which knocks over the other commandments. So the last commandment urges people to be content with what they have. Once envy is allowed to creep in, murder, adultery, theft and falsehood follow.

The desert of Sinai, where God's code of laws was set down for his people.

Saul

In fact, the reign of King Saul was a big disappointment. The pressures of leadership, coupled with disobedience to God and jealousy of the up-and-coming David, plunged him into bouts of depression. In the end, lonely and exhausted, he committed suicide during a battle with the Philistines.

David

It was under Saul's successor, King David (of Goliath fame!), that Israel enjoyed the finest period of its history.

Over a period of forty years, David established Jerusalem as the nation's capital, and so linked together two key traditions: the idea that Mount Zion (Jerusalem) is God's geographical centre, and the divine promise that David's kingdom would last for ever.

David succeeded in uniting all the tribes of Israel for the first time, and extended the borders of the kingdom so that they actually occupied all the land God had promised to Abraham. All in all, a state of affairs which had never existed before, and has never been repeated since.

In addition, David's whole approach to government was God-centred. It was the Lord who reigned, with the king as his representative on earth.

Solomon

David was succeeded by his son Solomon, who built the temple, fostered the Jewish culture, and expanded trade.

But his schemes were expensive, and resulted in heavy taxation and rampant inflation. And despite his wisdom, Solomon was a fool when it came to women. He broke God's law by contracting marriages outside Israel—'seven hundred princesses and three hundred concubines'—and so invited a foreign army of attractive pagans to take up residence in his palace. Of course, they brought their idols with them, and Solomon was soon found among the worshippers. The heritage of David—the relationship of God's people—was about to disintegrate.

Decline and fall

After Solomon, Israel split into two kingdoms—Israel in the north, and Judah in the south. In the centuries that followed, the two states were increasingly buffeted by the power politics of neighbouring empires. In the end, the northern kingdom fell to the Assyrians in 722BC and the population was entirely dispersed. The southern kingdom lingered on for a while, but was eventually overrun by the Babylonians. Jerusalem, the southern capital, fell in 587BC, and most of the people were carried off to exile in Babylon.

Exile

There followed a tremendous crisis of faith for the Jews. They had assumed that God would never let them down, because they were his people. They lived in his land, worshipped in his holy temple, and were ruled by his king...

Now the promised land was desolate, Jerusalem and the temple were in ruins, and their king was a captive in a foreign prison.

New hope

However, through the faithful work of the prophets, God taught his people that he still had a future for them. The exile was his judgment on their sin. But in his good time he would lead them back to their land, and give them a new start.

In 538BC an edict of the Persian Emperor Cyrus allowed the Jews to return to their own country. During the course of the next century, under the leadership of such men as Nehemiah and Ezra, the temple was rebuilt and the walls of Jerusalem restored.

THE PROPHETS

The men who kept hope alive through the dark days of siege, destruction and deportation were the prophets.

In the days of Samuel, prophets were called 'seers'. They had some kind of God-given intuition, or second sight, which enabled them to 'see'. Anything from lost property to the will of God for his people!

In due course, the prophets emerged as God's messengers. The first to have his words recorded was Amos, as he attacked the people of the northern kingdom. There was, he said, a credibility gap between their worship and their way of life:

The Lord says, 'I hate your religious festivals; I cannot stand them! When you bring me burnt offerings, I will not accept them; I will not accept the animals you have fattened to bring me as offerings. Stop your noisy songs; I do not want to listen to your harps. Instead, let justice flow like a stream, and righteousness like a river that never goes dry.'

However, when all was lost, with Israel dispersed and Judah in exile, it was the prophets who assured the survivors of God's continuing love. Through their preaching, the Jews realized that the Living God was not limited to geographical boundaries. He was Lord of the whole world, the whole universe. His judgment had fallen on them because their public and private lives had been a scandal: an affront to his holiness.

The prophecies of Jeremiah, Ezekiel, and the later chapters of Isaiah spoke of a future in which God's rule would be established on earth, and his righteousness would be written in people's hearts.

Prophecy is a phenomenon unique in Judaism and Christianity. The curious, compelling mixture of foretelling and forthtelling has no parallel in any other religion or philosophy.

Most fascinating of all are the Old Testament prophecies, uttered by many different people over hundreds of years, which build up a picture of the future Christ:

- **It was prophesied that the coming of the Messiah would be preceded by a prophet** preparing the way.

- He would be born of a young woman in the small town of Bethlehem.

- He would be betrayed for thirty pieces of silver which would be used to purchase a certain field.

- He would be crucified—a death most movingly described in Psalm 22.

- He would rise from the dead.

*But he endured the suffering that
    should have been ours,
    the pain that we should have borne.
All the while we thought that his
    suffering
was punishment sent by God*

*But because of our sins he was
    wounded,
    beaten because of the evil we did.
We are healed by the punishment he
    suffered,
    made whole by the blows he
    received.
All of us were like sheep that were
    lost,
    each of us going his own way.
But the Lord made the punishment
    fall on him,
    the punishment all of us deserved.*

THE BOOK OF ISAIAH

After that, the prophetic voice falls silent for six hundred years—until the time of Jesus.

POWER FOR LIFE

In the Bible, the Spirit is there at the very beginning, 'moving over the water', in the beautiful Genesis account of creation.

But the Holy Spirit is a person—not an 'it'! He is as personal as God the Father and God the Son.

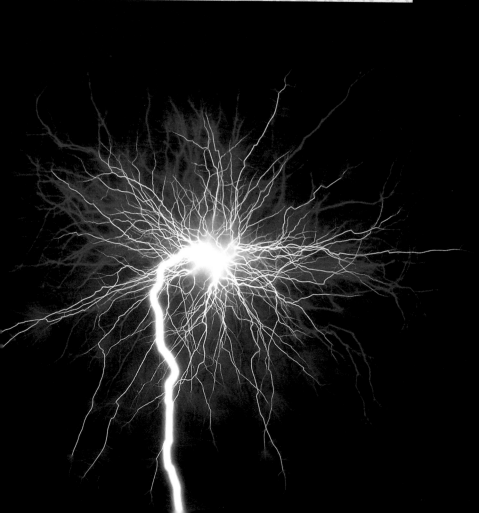

THAT'S THE SPIRIT

As the story of God's people unfolds, the Spirit makes an occasional appearance—empowering great leaders, inspiring prophets. But always there is a sense of spiritual 'rationing'. Of the thousands of people who pass before us in the pages of the Old Testament, only a few are allowed the power and presence of God's Spirit. And even for them, it is a fleeting and infrequent experience.

But the prophet Joel looked forward to something better. Through him, God said,

Afterwards I will pour out my Spirit on everyone: your sons and daughters will proclaim my message; your old men will have dreams, and your young men will see visions. At that time I will pour out my Spirit even on servants, both men and women.

When Jesus came, the Spirit of God was the whole dynamic of his life. He was conceived by the power of the Holy Spirit. The Spirit descended on him at his baptism, and was active throughout his ministry. 'The Spirit of the Lord is upon me,' said Jesus, quoting the prophet Isaiah, at the outset of his ministry. And after Jesus died on the cross, it was the Spirit of God who raised him from death.

On the night of his arrest, when Jesus and his disciples were at supper, he assured them he would send the Spirit to them, after he had gone.

The Spirit would keep them company, just as Jesus had done. But while Jesus was limited by a human body, the Spirit would be with each of them all the time, wherever they were.

Like Jesus, the Spirit would reveal the truth about God. He would challenge the world's values

Divine united

In the Bible, God is seen at work in three ways.

God the Father gets things going. It is he who does the creative planning. It is he who made the universe and surrounds it with his love.

God the Son, Jesus Christ, was sent by the Father to be the Saviour of the world. Completely human yet fully divine, his task and achievement was to be the agent not only of creation but also of a whole new creation.

God the Holy Spirit is, as it were, the executive branch—the one who does the work! Through him the Father and the Son are present and active in the world in general and in the church in particular.

Three distinct persons, each divine, and uniquely united. This 'three-in-one' understanding of God is known as 'the Trinity'.

of right and wrong, convince people of God's truth, and promote the Good News of Christ.

All in all, the Holy Spirit can be understood as the Spirit of Jesus, living in his followers and continuing his work.

On the Day of Pentecost, the Holy Spirit was freely poured out on humankind for the first time in history. As the crowds came rushing together to find out what was going on, Peter explained that Joel's prophecy was being fulfilled before their eyes. The climate had changed to 'Spirit' and he greeted it like the arrival of spring. It was an end to rationing!

The Holy Spirit is the life support of the Christian church: he provides the wherewithal for serving Christ, knitting the church together, and equipping it to spread the gospel.

The Spirit's gifts are given to individuals for the benefit of all. They range from inspired messages of wisdom or special insight, through powers of caring, teaching and healing, to the ability to speak in strange tongues. Some gifts are exciting and exotic; others are plain, practical and down to earth. Taken together, they enable a church to support one another and communicate the gospel.

While spiritual gifts may vary from person to person, the fruit of the Spirit is always the same. It is the opposite of selfishness. Paul describes it as 'love, joy, peace, patience, kindness, goodness, faithfulness, humility, and self-control'.

These are not separate qualities,

The church: who is it for?

When Groucho Marx was asked why he didn't belong to any clubs, he replied that he would never join a club which would have someone like him as a member!

In the Christian church, the opposite is the case. The church is a gathering of sinful men and women who would never have qualified to have anything to do with God, except that Jesus Christ has invited them to come to him, and they have accepted.

To this very day, the church exists for those outside it: those who are sinners, and know it, and want God to forgive them through Christ and make them his children.

to be collected like stamps. They are the many aspects of a believer's life when the Spirit is truly present. Eloquence and ecstasy are all very well, but without 'fruit' they are just a noise.

Perhaps the most wonderful of all, from the believer's point of view, is the sense of freedom and belonging that the Spirit gives. It is by the Spirit's power that we call Jesus our Lord, and God our Father. And he helps us when we pray, pleading with God for us in ways too deep for words.

THE BODY ON THE GROUND

The church is people

When the New Testament talks of the church, it never means a large building with stained-glass windows and a spire. On the contrary, it is always referring to a gathering of believers.

The true, total church includes all those who belong to Christ both on earth and in heaven. It is the longest-running multi-racial and multi-cultural society ever known.

The church is also the local group, large or small, which meets

---

Pictures of the church

The church is described in various ways in the New Testament.

Church members are like citizens of a kingdom

Jesus himself hardly mentioned the church at all. But he talked about 'the kingdom of God' a hundred times. The kingdom was the 'new society' which Jesus came to create. The full power and glory of God's kingdom are still in the future but true Christians belong to the kingdom, work for it, pray for it, and look for its fulfilment.

Church members are like a building

Both Peter and Paul knew that the church is made up of people. Yet they drew on the idea of a physical building to describe it.

Peter urged Christians to let God build them together, using them like 'living stones' in his 'spiritual temple'. The keystone, of course, is Jesus Christ—an idea echoed by Paul. (Or maybe he thought of it first!)

for worship and scatters for service.

There is, and has always been, an 'overlap' of those who really belong to Christ and are members of the true, total church, and those who are 'just looking' and have joined a particular local church as enquirers. So what signs mark those who belong?

- **They have completely committed themselves to Jesus Christ, put their trust in him as their Saviour, and obey him as their Lord.**

- **Their baptism (an outer wash) is matched by a heart-felt repentance and an open and public belief in Jesus.**

Church members are like a body

Paul's finest picture of the church is to describe it as 'the body of Christ'. Every believer is like a part of the body—every part different, but indispensable to the rest.

With a nice touch of humour, Paul points out that an eye is very different from a foot, but neither can get along very well without the other. So it is with the body of Christ.

A converted Jewish Pharisee may seem to have little in common with a converted Roman slave. But by the very fact that they both call Jesus 'Lord', they have the greatest unity in the world. Christians, says Paul, are like a body. And Jesus himself is its head.

The church is like a bride

At one point, Paul talks of the church being loved by Christ in the same way as a husband loves his wife. Jesus loved his people before ever they loved him. He came to give his life for them. He came to make them beautiful. They, in turn, should give him their complete devotion.

- **They let the Holy Spirit change their lives, through the wonder of worship, the example of Jesus, and the loving support of other believers.**

THE CHRISTIAN DIFFERENCE

Jesus described his followers as 'the salt of the earth'.

In those days, salt was used as a fertilizer. It was spread on the fields to promote good growth. It was also used as a disinfectant; sprinkled as necessary to kill off the bugs!

For us today, salt is something which gives flavour. It has a tang and kick to it which makes food tasty.

Again, until recently, it was widely used as a preservative—rubbed into meat and fish to arrest decay.

So what differences does Christ look for in his salty followers?

He looks for holiness

In Jesus' day the Pharisees expressed their holiness by keeping 248 commandments and 365 prohibitions. Jesus calls his followers to an even *greater* righteousness. A purity of faith and life which soars above the shackles and pitfalls of legalism. Holiness basically means being 'set apart' for God, dedicated to him.

He looks for love

The old law had commanded people to love their neighbours. But that had allowed them to continue to hate their enemies. Jesus said there was only one thing to do with enemies, and that was love them! In the vocabulary of God, your neighbour *includes* your enemy. Jesus taught his disciples to love one another, love their enemies, and do good to those who hated them. His followers today must do the same.

He looks for worship

True worship comes from the heart. A mechanical murmuring of prayers, or mindless singing of hymns, can actually *prevent* a person meeting with God. Indeed, Malcolm Muggeridge once accused the church of providing a refuge for those who are avoiding God!

Real worship wells up from inside us, released by the Holy Spirit. As Jesus said, 'God is Spirit, and only by the power of his Spirit can people worship him as he really is.'

He looks for freedom

Jesus came to set people free from the slavery of self-centredness. He told his followers not to be eaten up with anxiety about money, possessions or security. They could safely trust God for their every need.

So the Christian is set free. But the new freedom is for service: the service of God through serving others. Jesus said, 'Be concerned above everything else with the kingdom of God and with what he requires of you, and he will provide you with all these other things.'

Why different churches?

There are many different 'flavours' of Christian church to choose from.

Usually, the differences arose through disagreements over points of teaching. For example, Baptists are so called because they only baptize adult believers, while Anglicans are prepared to baptize the children of believing parents.

Other differences arise because tastes vary. Quiet, reflective people may like formal 'Prayer Book' services, or Quaker silence; while exuberant extroverts might opt for the informality and zest of Pentecostal worship.

In all this, there is a basic unity of faith between all true Christians. God has made people, nations and cultures in splendid variety. We should not be too alarmed when we find this wealth expressed in different styles of worship or church organization.

PRAYER

Great men and women of God have always had lives rooted in prayer.

You can't say 'some prayed and some didn't', because they all did! Prayer is a fact of the Christian life. A fact, not a feeling.

Prayer puts God at the centre

It is as though we leave the stage of our own life, and take a seat in the audience instead. And then we look at that stage from God's point of view, and ask him to occupy the centre and receive the glory.

Prayer is costly

It is costly in time and effort. But more than that, it is costly in its implications. We can't say to God, 'Your will be done on earth' without being prepared to be caught up in the consequences of that prayer. We ask God to feed the hungry, help the weak, and comfort the sad. No sooner have we made the request, than there comes into our mind an awareness of the hungry, needy, and sad people we know. The prayer is to be answered, in part at least, through us!

Prayer is getting involved with God

It is for those who are prepared to have God change their mind. It is not a cheap way of having a good conscience, by asking him to rubber-stamp the decisions we have already made. Nor is it a matter of God putting a tick in the margin of our common sense. It is seeking

God's will, and wrestling to steer his course in the tempest of events.

That means listening as well as talking. And it's more than 'God bless Granny and make her good'!

Prayer is wholehearted commitment

When the risen Christ spoke to the Christians at Laodicea, he revealed his hatred of indifference:

I know that you are neither cold nor hot. How I wish you were either one or the other! But because you are lukewarm, neither hot nor cold, I am going to spit you out of my mouth!

Genuine prayer is often hard. It is also, at heart, very simple—and radically serious. In praying, we talk to God confidentially and reverently, like children to a parent. And by praying, we bring to him the whole of our life, and the whole of our world, for his blessing.

Prayer is joy

In prayer we find a new lease of life. We realize that the God who made us also loves us. We realize that everything is in his control, and we can tackle the problems of life in his strength.

We realize that there is time to do everything that he wants us to do. We can savour each moment and relish each encounter, because they are God-given. We praise God for his world. We rejoice in it, and have hope for the future.

The prayer life of Jesus

Jesus was a man with a lot to do and very little time in which to do it. Yet he had time to wine and dine and laugh and share stories.

He knew that very soon he must go to Jerusalem to suffer and die. Yet he poured his life into the needs of others, patiently accepting each urgent interruption and setting people free in body and mind.

We never feel that Jesus was putting on an act. There was no other side to him. He never tried to live up to other people's expectations. He didn't manipulate people, treating them as 'contacts' to be used. Nor did he try to possess or smother people, imposing on them the burden of his own emotional needs.

Although he came to change the world, he didn't overwork! It's true that on occasions he got up early, or missed a meal, or fell asleep from exhaustion. But surely these occasions are mentioned because they are the exception rather than the rule . . .

In everything he had integrity. He cared nothing for class distinction or accent. He was not impressed by power or worldly position. When he was angry, he was 'perfectly' angry—not over-reacting in a fit of pique. When he challenged the divisions and delusions of society, he did so out of love—love for the unlovely outsider, *and* the crabby insider.

Finally, as he gave up his life on the cross, he was able to shout 'It is finished!' It was an extraordinary claim to make. No doubt there were still people with leprosy, those crippled and on crutches, and women on the streets. There were certainly shortsighted and blinkered scholars, still picking over the bones of the Law. But the work of Jesus was 'finished'. He had done the work his Father sent him to do. No more and no less.

How did Jesus come by such insight and balance?

His secret was prayer.

In prayer, Jesus realized he was God's Son. He basked in the relation-ship, calling God 'Abba' —the first word uttered by a Hebrew child: 'Dad'.

For Jesus, prayer was like a good meal. He felt nourished. Well fed. Complete. He spoke of 'abiding' in the Father. Prayer charged his batteries and gave him power for life.

In prayer, Jesus realized his mission. His Father had sent him to be the light of the world, the living bread, the water of life . . .

He knew also that he was the Suffering Servant, the Lamb of God, born to bear the sin of the world.

Knowing who he was, and realizing what he had to do, Jesus embarked on his life's work. In so doing, he did not leave prayer behind. For him, prayer was as vital as breathing. And so, from time to time, he would turn aside from the clamour of people's demands, and refresh himself in the Father's love.

For Jesus, prayer was nothing less than a relationship. A way of life.

When we pray to God, we are not approaching a remote unknowable force, but a supremely generous father.

PRAYER: DO IT YOURSELF

Begin with God

Pause. Remember that he is Creator and Lord. Remember that he is holy, and ask his forgiveness of the wrong things in your life. Remember that he is Father, concerned to listen to the stumbling words of his child.

'Pull yourself together'

Think of the main aspects of your life (those you love, the demands of home and work, your hopes and frustrations) and draw them together before God. This avoids the hypocrisy of holding a polite conversation with God in, as it were, the smart front room of your life, while barricading him away from the secrets of the kitchen and the horrors of the store room!

Remember Jesus

For Jesus, prayer was a way of life. It was a relaxing in the Father's love, a fresh commitment to the work of his kingdom.

Remember the Spirit

'The Spirit comes to help us, weak as we are, for we do not know how we ought to pray; the Spirit himself pleads with God for us in groans that words cannot express.'

Ask God to catch up your prayer in the prayer of the Spirit.

Be secret

Jesus taught that prayer is essentially private, between you and God. 'When you pray,' he said, 'go to your room, close the door, and pray to your Father, who is unseen.'

Be honest

When we come to God in prayer, we come as we *are*. There is no point at all in trying to come as we aren't! God does not judge us by what we are pretending to be, or by what other people think us to be. He knows us through and through. And he loves us all the same!

Worship is the submission of all our nature to God: the quickening of our conscience by his holiness, the nourishment of our mind with his truth, the purifying of our imagination by his beauty, the opening of the heart to his love, the surrender of will to his purpose and all this gathered up in adoration.
WILLIAM TEMPLE

Be brief

When we pray, there are no marks for long words, and no bonus points for overtime. Indeed, it is interesting to note that when Jesus taught his disciples a prayer, it was quite short. Think before you pray; don't be afraid to come to the point, and pray 'little and often'—at least to begin with. And finally,

Be thankful

Thankfulness is the keynote to which we tune our prayers. As Paul says: 'Don't worry about anything, but in all your prayers ask God for what you need, always asking him with a thankful heart.'

Wonder, love and praise

The greatest thing in the church's life is worship.

Just as men and women are most fully human when they respond to God's love, so the church is most fully itself when its members combine to give glory to God.

Worship is an opening of our lives to God, like flowers to the sun. It is as if we move towards God to embrace him and enjoy his company.

But it is also costly. Just as the Jews gave the first and best of their animals to God for sacrifice, so Christians seek to offer themselves to him as completely as possible. After all, if worship costs nothing, the chances are it is worth nothing.

Worship is 'giving God his worth'. We praise him out of gratitude that he has made us, and that he has saved us through Christ.

Worship is a celebration of our freedom. Jesus has won forgiveness for our sins, broken the fetters of legalism, and even conquered death. Better still, God has adopted us, and we can call him 'Father'.

Worship is involvement with others. Christians belong to each other in the Body of Christ, sharing and serving together. Each member has a different gift, and everyone is needed if the Body is to be healthy, active and effective. It follows that it's impossible to worship God and ignore other Christians, though many people attempt it!

Worship is often emotional, naturally enough. If football supporters can get excited about their team, how much more can rescued sinners enthuse about their Saviour! Again, simply to be alive, awake, and aware of God's love is enough to make the soul take flight. As the hymn says:

When all thy mercies, O my God,
My rising soul surveys:
Transported with the view, I'm lost
In wonder, love and praise.

THE OTHER SIDE OF THE COIN

There is one problem to which any thoughtful person returns time and again. If the universe was created by a loving and all-powerful God, why is there so much suffering in the world?

THE UGLY TRUTH

When we see the devastating effects of natural disasters, babies born with desperate disabilities, tyrants plunging their people into war, we can't help but puzzle over God's role in it all. Perhaps God is well-meaning, and loves us, but this world has long since escaped from his control. Or perhaps he is not as strong as we thought.

Needless to say, there are no easy answers to such questions. But at least Christianity recognizes the *fact* of suffering. It makes sense both of the glory and of the failure of the world in a way true of no other belief. And, above all, Jesus has himself taken responsibility for the sin and suffering of the world.

The Bible certainly recognizes the fact of suffering. In the Old Testament, the history of Israel includes times of national crisis and disaster. The people experience slavery in Egypt, sickness and death in the wilderness, and, many centuries later, the fall of Jerusalem and exile in Babylon.

In the New Testament we read of a Messiah who was crucified after betrayal by a close friend, and rejection by the people. The early Christians suffered attempts at intimidation, as well as outright persecution and imprisonment.

What can we say? There are at least some pointers to go by.

Suffering and evil go together

When God created the world, everything was perfect. Humankind was in harmony with God, and was free to explore and enjoy the world. This is the story of Adam and Eve in the Garden of Eden.

When God made human beings, he gave them free will

Quite apart from the instincts and reflexes which they share with the rest of the animal kingdom, humans have a unique freedom to obey or disobey God. The ugly truth is that, right from the beginning, men and women have rebelled against God, and every single person born into this world has a character marred by selfishness and pride.

This selfishness the Bible calls 'sin'—a spoiling, spreading disease of the spirit which inevitably separates human beings from a holy God; and as a result from one another, too.

In the story of Adam and Eve, the Bible tells how the whole creation was flawed when God and humankind became enemies. Human relationships were undermined by recrimination and lies. Life became a battle for survival, scratching a living from the soil. Childbirth became difficult, and death was certain.

True love always risks rejection

When God made human beings, he hoped for a loving relationship. But love is only real if it is freely offered. So God made them with both a capacity to love and a freedom to choose. In other words, we aren't robots or puppets whose responses can be dictated or programmed in advance.

When people choose to reject God's love, suffering and death are the inevitable result. They are 'the other side' of the coin of free will. They are the shadow cast by love.

Sin is deeply ingrained in human nature

Paul wrote to the Christians at Rome: 'Everyone has sinned and is far away from God's saving presence.' All too often, we sin not because we choose to but because we can't help it.

Nor is there anything that we can do by way of 'turning over a new leaf', or 'trying to be good', which will make any difference. Sin is a well-established cancer which no amount of external scrubbing can remove.

The astonishing message of the

Can God redeem suffering?

In some ways, the answer is yes:

Suffering can turn us to God. If life were like a primrose path, there would be no problems to face, and no difficulties to endure. It would no doubt be harmlessly pleasant, but there would be little to develop our character! Certainly we would have no need of God.

But when trouble strikes, or illness—the things over which we have no control—then we find ourselves asking God for his help. We may feel hypocritical, especially if God has heard precious little from us before. Nevertheless, he quickly answers those who truly seek him.

Suffering can turn us to others. Sometimes we are shaken from our complacency by a picture of a starving child, or the need of a disabled neighbour. Their suffering awakens in us a desire to help as best we can.

C.S. Lewis described pain as 'God's megaphone to rouse a deaf world'. Time and again, through our own suffering or that of others, we are thrown into a far more wonderful relationship with people than we could ever have known otherwise.

Suffering can refine us. It is simply not true that God's people lead a charmed life. On the contrary, some of those who have been closest to God have also known the deepest suffering. St Teresa of Avila once said: 'I do not wonder, God, that you have so few friends—from the way you treat them!'

In the letter to the Hebrews, the writer says, 'Even though Jesus was God's Son, he learned through his sufferings to be obedient.' Somehow suffering can deepen trust in God.

Then again, there is something about suffering patiently borne which brings healing, peace, and new perspective, to others. It is part of what Jesus was doing on the cross: 'Christ also suffered for sins, the just for the unjust, that he might bring us to God.'

Bible is that God has done something about the problem of evil.

He has given his Son to die for the sin of the world. Through the cross of Jesus, God himself experienced the reality of pain and suffering.

Suffering and death are the result of human sinfulness. In the case of Jesus, it was not *his* sin for which he died but *ours*. He took down into death all our frustrations and agony and alienation from God.

We can go free!

From the inside, from a person's heart, come the evil ideas which lead him to do immoral things, to rob, kill, commit adultery, be greedy, and do all sorts of evil things; deceit, indecency, jealousy, slander, pride, and folly—all these evil things come from inside a person and make him unclean.

JESUS, IN THE GOSPEL OF MARK

In his death, Jesus was a 'black hole' for the sins of the world. He did not retaliate, setting up ripples of revenge. Instead, he accepted the rage and spite, and took it out of circulation. This is a function his followers continue to have, if they endure the pain of undeserved suffering.

It is a great mystery that the suffering which God never intended is not only *allowed* by him, but is even used for his glory. It makes us question the meaning of life and perhaps discover, through our own agony, the suffering love of God.

SATAN AND THE OCCULT

God has an enemy. His name is Satan.

Satan (which means 'Adversary') appears in the Bible as the chief rebel against God. Jesus encounters him in a very personal way, quite apart from the dealings he had with many lesser demons.

The Bible teaches that Satan is not on a par with God. He is an angel, created by God, who turned against his Maker in pride and jealousy.

It was Satan (in the story of Adam and Eve) who tempted humankind to disobey God; and from earliest times he has been active in defacing creation and degrading human life. Jesus had no hesitation in describing Satan as 'the ruler of this world', and the temptation to compromise or collaborate with him was apparently very real.

In the Bible, Satan is variously described as 'the Evil One", 'a slanderer', and 'the father of lies'. He seeks to challenge and undermine trust in God, persuading people to doubt his power and love, and plunging them into depression.

But Satan is a defeated foe. His stranglehold on this world was decisively broken through the death of Christ on the cross. The war between God and the devil continues throughout the period known as 'the Last Days'—hence the many situations which are so obviously Satan-inspired and controlled. But, thanks to the cross, sin and guilt can

be dealt with, and the fear and finality of death has been brought to an end. As a result, Satan's power-base has been demolished, and his time grows short.

Committed Christians are all too aware that they are part of a spiritual battle of cosmic dimensions. Paul wrote to the Christians at Ephesus (the letter to the Ephesians):

Put on all the armour that God gives you, so that you will be able to stand up against the devil's evil tricks. For we are not fighting against human beings but against the wicked spiritual forces in the heavenly world, the rulers, authorities, and

*all the burning arrows shot by the
Evil One. And accept salvation as a
helmet, and the word of God as the
sword which the Spirit gives you.*

The occult

The power of Satan is clearly seen
when people engage in occult
practices.

The 'occult' means that which is
hidden or kept secret. It can include
the thoughts of other people,
warning of future events, or
information concerning the dead.
Today the influence of the occult is
vast, ranging from astrology and
fortune-telling to black magic and
witchcraft.

There is even a revival of interest
in the myths of bygone ages. There
is no shortage of books on
mysterious centres such as
Stonehenge and Glastonbury, or the
influence of the signs of the Zodiac.
And the *I Ching*, or Chinese 'Book of
Changes', has taken a firm hold on
many who seek spirit-guidance.

Even on an apparently harmless
level, people 'keep their fingers
crossed' or 'touch wood'. And who
can resist a glance at 'What the Stars
Foretell' in a newspaper or maga-
zine? After all, they are very often
right...

All these activities are in fact the
thin end of Satan's wedge. They are
anti-God. Acting as psychic drugs,
they begin with curiosity, establish
dependence, and then produce fear,
depression, and even death.

*cosmic powers of this dark age. So
put on God's armour now! Then
when the evil day comes, you will be
able to resist the enemy's attacks;
and after fighting to the end, you will
still hold your ground.*

In the same letter, Paul described
God-given spiritual weapons in
terms of a Roman soldier's
equipment:

*So stand ready, with truth as a belt
tight around your waist, with
righteousness as your breastplate,
and as your shoes the readiness to
announce the Good News of peace.
At all times carry faith as a shield;
for with it you will be able to put out*

OTHER FAITHS

Christianity is not the only religion in the world. There are other great faiths, each with millions of followers, which also claim to reveal the truth about God!

What's more, through business and travel, college life and the media, the different religions are rubbing shoulders as never before. This raises questions.

- **Aren't all religions very much the same?**

- **What's so special about Jesus?**

Deep in humanity's nature is the need to worship

Every community in every age has had ways of reckoning with the invisible. Holy places abound, with holy people to guard their secrets. Shrines have developed and become places of pilgrimage. Temples and churches have been built—places of refuge and inspiration in a world of relentless change. Taken together, all this is massive evidence that human beings have an in-built longing for God.

In many parts of the world, the modern gods are materialism, security and success. There is also an obsession with sex—a demand for personal sexual fulfilment, and a preoccupation with the behaviour of others (especially the famous!). Such gods (and goddesses) have in fact been in business for centuries, and people of many ages and cultures have gladly sacrificed their lives in their service.

The great religions share some common ground

Judaism, Islam and Christianity share common roots. In varying degrees they look to Abraham as their founding father. They share the belief that God created the universe. They hold that God has made himself known through prophets and scripture, and they look for the resurrection of the dead and God's final judgment.

Many of the great religions set standards for human behaviour

Ever since Confucius, there has been a principle of 'do as you would be done by'. But at this point a gap begins to show between Christianity and the rest. Other religions are ways of getting to God by *trying*. Trying to be holy. Trying to be good.

Hindus seek to achieve detachment from the world and to attain the blessedness of union with Brahman, the changeless Being which upholds and indwells the universe. One method they use is Yoga: a combination of physical self-control and mental poise and concentration.

Buddhism teaches that there is a Way by which we can free ourselves from the passions and desires which are the cause of suffering. It is called the Noble Eightfold Path, and its self-denial and self-discipline lead in the end to enlightenment and to Nirvana. Following the Way involves a supreme effort of self-control.

Islam lays great emphasis on submission to God, lived out through set forms of prayer every day, giving to charity, pilgramage to holy places and fasting. The Muslim is saved through doing these good works and will be judged on them after death.

The essence of Christianity, on the other hand, is *trust*. Christians trust that, on the cross, Jesus Christ did all that was necessary to secure forgiveness and new life for lost humankind. 'Doing good' is certainly an important *outcome* of knowing God's love, but it is most emphatically *not* the means by which we *earn* God's love.

Christianity reveals that God has reached out to his world in the life and death of his Son. At the resurrection, a bridgehead was established across which God and human beings could be reunited. This is very different from other religions, which practise the 'bootstrap' principle of trying to haul themselves up to God by constant effort and self-denial.

In fact, if a 'religion' is a system whereby men and women achieve their salvation, then Christianity doesn't qualify! It fails on the grounds that God's salvation in Christ is not something that can be worked for. It simply has to be accepted.

So are the followers of other religions on the right side of God or not?

Of course there is truth to be found in other religions. It would be surprising if there weren't. But the more we look at other religions, the clearer it becomes that Jesus Christ is unique. The teachings of Muhammad, Buddha or Confucius do not stand or fall on the character and integrity of their founders. With Christianity, it is Jesus himself who is all-important. He once described himself as 'the way, the truth and the life'—or in other words the true and living way to God.

This means that Jesus is in fact far greater than even Christians can realize or imagine. He is the Beginning and End of everything— the focal point of heaven and earth, time and eternity.

So when people in other faiths respond to the light of God in their own religion, it is Jesus they are beginning to glimpse. And it is in Jesus that their longings will be fulfilled.

In his life and death, Jesus revealed God in a very complete way. Indeed, some leading members of other faiths have been greatly attracted to Christ, but sadly disillusioned by what they saw of his church! All the same, when Christ appears in glory, all those who have searched longingly for God will find their fulfilment in him.

Why atheists?

In the last century there has been a widespread rejection of God in many parts of the world. Many people will state quite bluntly that they are 'atheists': they do not believe in God. Other, more cautious, or simply trying to hedge their bets, will describe themselves as 'agnostic': they just do not know. There are many good reasons for their point of view.

- 'Science has disproved religion'

Ever since Galileo dared to suggest that the world was round, religion and science have tended to get the wrong side of each other. Of course, many of the great scientists were Christians, and still are. But the old medieval world-view—heaven 'up there' and hell 'down there', was a long time dying, to say nothing of the belief that God had created the universe in six days flat. Overall, it seemed that the Bible was hostile to reason and science, and in turn reason and science laid siege to the Bible.

- 'Why does God allow war?'

If God is alive and well, say the atheists, why does he not step in to avert suffering and disaster? Many of those who went to fight in two World Wars had their faith shattered and returned disillusioned with the whole idea of a personal and loving God.

- 'God is out of touch!'

With concerns about the environment, mass unemployment, Aids and the breakdown of social structures, many people wonder what hope there is for the world. Science is a powerful resource, but it isn't the same as God. It causes as many problems as it solves.

What evidence is there that anyone can solve the problems of our complex world, or that God can be involved in such a mess?

- 'We don't need God any more'

In ancient times, God was the best hope in everything from cultivating the crop to bearing healthy babies. But gradually, as the jigsaw of human knowledge and achievement was built up, God was no longer needed in matters of food and fertility.

Nowadays, humans seem able to control everything—with the possible exception of the weather. Illness is dealt with at the health centre; depression is lifted by the psychiatrist.

- 'Religion is a con'

In many places, the institutional church has been thrown out, along with the government. Revolutionaries opposed belief in God because religion had been used to suppress freedom and progress. The church had been a pillar of the establishment, preserving the position of the privileged. Karl Marx accused religion of being 'the opiate of the people'—drugging and deluding them to keep them in their place.

- 'The church is full of hypocrites'

Some people dismiss God by referring to the poor track-record of his church. They respect Christ and his teaching, but find no image or echo of him in the life of their local congregation.

So what?!

Do any or all of these arguments disprove the existence of God?
Not at all!

Science

There is no basic conflict between science and the Bible. Modern science was born and developed largely by committed Christians. It was belief in a personal God as Creator that encouraged them to look for order and meaning in the universe.

The 'Darwin versus creation' struggle has gone on for many years, but the battle is not just a matter of science versus religion. 'Evolution' now is not often the same total philosophy of life it was once held to be. If it is part of the mechanism God used in creation, Christians can give God glory for the wonderful things science has discovered—as well as for the unique relationship between God and humanity which has been made possible by Christ.

Suffering

The problems of suffering will always provide the atheist with ample ammunition. But as well as the problem of evil, we have a problem of good! How do we account for love, security, happiness, and meaning? The philosopher Emmanuel Kant said, 'God's existence is unprovable—but so is atheism.' Christianity makes sense of the fact both of good *and* evil.

Exploitation

Karl Marx was quite right in suggesting that religion can be used to exploit people. It certainly was, but it needn't be. A living faith in God can bring freedom and fulfilment to both individuals and nations. Perhaps today materialism is an opiate of the people.

• Can a thoughtful person believe in God? The answer is 'yes'. And they won't have to commit intellectual suicide or make a blind leap of faith of do so.

Committed belief arises from deep thought. Those who have faith are not going gainst reason or experience. On the contrary, it is reason and experience which move us towards a faith.

Faith is reasonable in that it makes excellent sense of reality. It fits the facts.

THE SHAPE OF THINGS TO COME

Death is a fact of life.
It is an experience that every one of us will share.
We are born. We breathe, we eat, we sleep. And in the end, we die. But is it the end?
That's the question.

LIFE AFTER LIFE?

The behaviour of the early Christians at funerals was a scandal. For one thing, they wore white. For another, their tears of sadness were accompanied by an unmistakable note of joy!

They were absolutely certain that death is not the end. God has not made us in order to discard us like a paper cup. He wants us to know him and enjoy him for ever.

This life is not built to last. Our bodies grow old and die. Accident or illness can end our life at any time, and in a matter of minutes.

Christians believe that death is the threshold over which we go to be with God and share his eternal life. This revolutionary idea stemmed from the death and resurrection of Jesus. When God raised his Son from the tomb, the power and finality of death were broken. But it wasn't just Jesus who would emerge to a glorious new life on the other side of the grave. His victory was to be shared by his followers. Paul called Jesus 'the prototype'—the first of many.

The early Christians were already enjoying eternal life

Paul spoke of Christians being 'in Christ'. He had to bend the language to express the whole new dimension in which the believer lives. Belonging to Christ is a relationship with him which cannot be broken by death.

Death takes our friends *from* us, but it takes Christ's friends *to* him.

The apostles had already glimpsed the resurrection life

They had met with Jesus in his resurrection body. A body which was recognizably his, but no longer bound by the laws of nature. And they had received his assurances that eternal life was for them as well: 'Because I live, you will live also.'

When I die, I rot.
BERTRAND RUSSELL

Jesus said to Martha:
I am the resurrection and the life. Whoever believes in me will live, even though he dies; and whoever lives and believes in me will never die.
THE GOSPEL OF JOHN

SIGNS OF THE TIMES

Sooner or later, this world will come to an end.

Some people believe it will end with a bang: that we will destroy our precious earth by over-population, pollution, or nuclear war. The scientists know it is possible. The historians fear it is inevitable.

Some people think it will end with a whimper: that life will continue to evolve for millions of years to come, until the sun begins to die and life on earth becomes impossible. The astronomers know it is inevitable. The science fiction writers hope the human race will evacuate the planet and colonize the galaxy long before disaster strikes.

Christians hold a third view. They believe Jesus Christ will return to this earth as Judge and King.

When will it happen? Jesus said he did not know: 'No one knows when that day or hour will come—neither the angels in heaven, nor the Son; only the Father knows.' In the meantime:

There will be wars and revolutions

Jesus said, 'Countries will fight each other; kingdoms will attack one another.' He told his disciples not to be afraid when they heard of such things taking place.

There will be natural disasters

Jesus said, 'There will be terrible earthquakes, famines, and plagues everywhere; there will be strange and terrifying things coming from the sky.'

Christ's followers will be persecuted

Jesus told his disciples, 'You will be arrested and persecuted; you will be handed over to be tried in synagogues and be put in prison; you will be brought before kings and rulers for my sake.'

There will be false Messiahs

Jesus said, 'Many men, claiming to speak for me, will come and say, "I am he!" and, "The time has come!", but don't follow them.'

The last days

All these upheavals are symptoms of the Last Days. War, disaster, persecution and phoney religious leaders—these have been regular features of world news from the time of Jesus to the present day. And no doubt they will continue to be so until he comes again.

When are the Last Days?

They are *now*.

Jesus described the End Time in epic terms:

There will be strange things happening to the sun, the moon, and the stars. On earth whole countries will be in despair, afraid of the roar of the sea, and the raging tides. People will faint from fear as they wait for what is coming over the whole earth, for the powers in space will be driven from their courses. Then the Son of Man will appear, coming in a cloud with great power and glory. When these things begin to happen, stand up and raise your heads, because your salvation is near.

FROM LUKE'S GOSPEL

JESUS WILL COME AGAIN

What will it be like when Jesus Christ returns in glory?

Describing his return, Jesus drew on the cosmos-shaking images of what the Jews called 'the Day of the Lord':

After that time of trouble the sun will grow dark, the moon will no longer shine, the stars will fall from the heavens, and the powers in space will be driven from their courses. Then the Son of Man will appear, coming in the clouds with great power and glory. He will send the angels out to the four corners of the earth to gather God's chosen people from one end of the world to the other.

FROM MARK'S GOSPEL

Jesus told his disciples to be watchful and confident. There will be no need for panic or despair. God will bring down the curtain on the old order and bring in the new:

When you see these things happening, you will know that the Kingdom of God is about to come ... Be on the alert and pray always that you will have the strength to go safely through all those things that will happen and to stand before the Son of Man.

GOOD NEWS OF JUDGMENT

The world is moving towards a day when justice will be done—and will be seen to be done—by God.

Although the term 'last judgment' is never actually used in the Bible, there are powerful descriptions of 'the day of the Lord'. Paul frequently refers to 'that day' or 'the coming wrath'.

Jesus will be the Judge

Describing the events to his disciples, Jesus said, 'When the Son of Man comes as King and all the angels with him, he will sit on his royal throne, and the people of all the nations will be gathered before him ...'

It is response to Jesus that will count. It will be clearly seen that the whole of human life was an opportunity to respond to Christ. He

When will Christ come?

No one knows. Martin Luther wrote, 'The last day is near at hand.' That was in 1530.

George Whitefield, the great preacher, expected Jesus to come at any hour. He died in 1770.

Lord Shaftesbury, the social reformer, expected Jesus' return at any moment. He died in 1885.

Far from dismissing their insight, we should learn from their example. The fact of Christ's return gave energy and purpose to everything they did.

We, too, would do well to expect him 'soon'.

was involved in every encounter.

On judgment day, he will say to some: 'I was hungry and you fed me, thirsty and you gave me a drink; I was a stranger and you received me in your homes, naked and you clothed me; I was sick and you took care of me, in prison and you visited me.'

But to others, he will say: 'I was hungry but you would not feed me, thirsty but you would not give me a drink; I was a stranger but you would not welcome me in your homes . . . I tell you, whenever you refused to help one of these least important ones, you refused to help me.'

These words of Jesus reveal an astonishing fact. Final judgment is, in one sense, already here!

Whose choice?

Some people find the whole idea of judgment impossible to accept. Bertrand Russell, for example, thought it was a very tasteless form of blackmail: 'Religion is based, I think, primarily and mainly on fear. Fear is the parent of cruelty. And therefore it is no wonder if cruelty and religion go hand in hand.'

Of course, if we must obey or burn, we'll obey! But we will hardly respect a God who made up such an absurd game in the first place.

But there is another way of looking at it.

We live in a world of choice and consequence

Farmers know that if they want a good crop, they must sow good seed. If they want wheat, they must sow wheat. If they want barley, they must sow barley. They make the choice. They know the consequence.

In terms of behaviour, the same applies. Violence sown at the cinema or on television can lead to real-life violence on football terraces and city streets. Casual sex, sown in fantasy, can lead to the real-life agony of broken families and broken lives. Again, there is the principle of choice and consequence.

The Bible teaches that the whole of life 'adds up'

Everything we are, and everything we do, doesn't simply run down the plughole of the universe. It runs into the holiness and love of God.

And that's why judgment is good news:

● It's good news that God cares

He cares about the choices we make. He guides and encourages us by making the consequences clear. Like a loving father, he cares enough to reward our efforts and correct our mistakes.

● It's good news that evil will not triumph in the end

In our present state of affairs, good is not always rewarded, and wickedness is not always punished. For many people there is not a glimmer of fairness or justice in life from the moment they are born till the day they die. On judgment day, God will quite literally 'put everything right'.

● It's good news that the choice is ours

For those who have not yet responded to God's

It is our response to Christ in the present that decides our position in the future.

Judgment day isn't some terrible event descending on us out of the blue, and bearing no relation to anything that has gone before. On the contrary, it is an occasion when God will endorse, and make public, our own attitude to his Son.

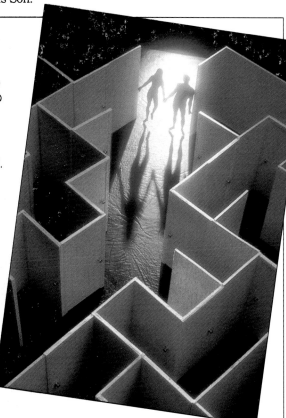

love in Jesus Christ, there is still time to change sides. In the terms of his parables, there's still time to accept the invitation to the banquet; still time to come to our senses and head for home.

Heaven is life with God. Hell is life without God. Heaven and hell are not rewards. They are the consequences of the choices we make.

God has done everything to ensure that we don't fall foul of his judgment. The most famous verse in the Bible sums it up:

God loved the world so much that he gave his only Son, so that every-one who believes in him may not die but have eternal life.

God has sent his Son to rescue and cleanse us from sin, so that we can stand acquitted before him.

He has done everything, that is, short of overriding our free will. And that means that, at the end of the day, the choice is ours.

89

A FAITH FOR ADULTS

The Christian faith is for people of all ages and
abilities. It can intrigue and absorb the finest mind,
yet it is simple enough for a child to understand.
And it takes account of the whole of life.

POWER AND PURPOSE

What we believe about God is the most important thing about us. It determines the overall direction of our life. It affects every action.

Many people will claim to believe in God, but a few minutes' conversation reveals that they really don't trust him an inch! Their life is totally geared to their own survival and security. Listen carefully and you hear the whine of self-pity, the hiss of jealousy, the rumble of anger, the purr of complacency... They believe in God, but he has not been allowed to engage or change their lives in the slightest degree.

Others will say, quite frankly, that they don't believe in God. They don't need any such prop or bolt-hole. But as you study their independence, you will notice gods of a sort: work, family, hobbies, possessions... No props? No bolt-holes?

Jesus came to give life. Full life. Abundant life. Life before death.

When we turn to Christ and follow him, our character and lifestyle start to be changed. Our old shape was moulded by selfishness and marred by sin. Our new shape is the likeness of Christ.

In some ways we don't change. The extrovert will still be an extrovert, though she may be easier to live with. The introvert will still be introspective, though he may well find it easier to live with himself.

In other ways we are radically different.

● **We enjoy a new freedom**

We are no longer the slaves of sin. We are free to do good.

● **We also enjoy a new power**

With God's Spirit in our lives, we are no longer shot through with fear. We don't have to spend time defending ourselves or justifying our actions. We know that we are accepted and loved by God, and therefore our energies are released for his service.

● **We begin to share God's concerns**

We become aware of the needs of others—the lonely, the sick, the disabled, the unemployed... We realize that many lives are in ruins, not because of their 'bad luck', but because of *our* greed and indifference. Like Little Jack Horner, we have kept to our cosy corner, stuffing ourselves with plum pie, and congratulating ourselves on being 'good'! Thanks to the coming of Jesus, we can see what goodness really looks like— and realize that we don't have it.

● **We start to be more open to others**

Before, we only made friends with people like ourselves ('birds of a feather flock together'), or with those we intended to exploit ('you scratch my back, I'll scratch yours'). We did this because other people were 'different' and made us feel

Pulling it together

We live in a world which is out of joint. We live in a scientific age, entirely dependent on the new technology for our future well-being; yet many are disillusioned with science. Science tells us what we *can* do; but it can't tell us what we *should* do. When it comes to moral values, we must look elsewhere.

We live in a self-confident age which is riddled with anxiety. People make up their own minds about sex outside marriage, homosexuality, abortion, and divorce. But for all the so-called freedom, they often find themselves bewildered and miserable. If there are no black-and-white standards, how is it we still feel guilty?

We live in a world of many choices. We can choose our values. We can choose our creed. Yet in a life of seventy or eighty years, most people don't give as much as ten minutes' thought to what they really believe. They settle for 'it doesn't matter, so long as you're sincere'. But what if they're sincerely wrong?

We live in a society where 'sex' and 'love' are regarded as meaning the same thing. Pop stars sing about it, film stars demonstrate it, and (according to the astrologers) the stars in the sky tell us when it's coming our way. But despite all this, an increasing number of people seem unable to build lasting, satisfying relationships. There is a lack of committed, reliable love. The kind of love which builds a home. The kind of love which provides children with a secure start in life. The kind of love which, if it doesn't exactly make the world go round, at least stops it falling apart.

In the West, we have a society which is materially rich, but spiritually bankrupt. Jesus summed up the conflict when he said, 'You *cannot* serve God and Mammon.' It simply can't be done. But we still try. It doesn't matter how many times the wealthy and the famous confess that money doesn't satisfy and that they have somehow 'missed out'. We still think we could make it work for us, given half a chance.

We live in a society in which people say they believe in God, but their faith has no relevance at all. By 'God' they mean an old man in the sky, who is short-sighted and slightly deaf, and who gives everyone the benefit of the doubt. If the Bible is right, they are in for a shock.

insecure in some way.

But now we find our prejudices crumbling. We don't need to hide behind a facade: we are free to be our real selves. We are not eaten up with jealousy or overcome with fear. Instead, we see other human beings whom God made and for whom Christ died. And we begin to extend to them something of the acceptance which we ourselves enjoy.

- **We also start to come alive in other ways**

Living whole

The greatest need we have—as individuals, as communities, as a world—is to 'get it all together'. We need 'wholeness'. We need 'health'. The Bible's word for it is 'holiness'.

We are quite wrong to think of a holy person as someone with a prayer book in one hand, a halo in the other and a benign smile on their face. Holiness is far more exciting than that. A holy person is a whole person—a person who is right with God, and who really makes the most of life, both for themself and others. But holiness is never the result of self-improvement. It comes only from knowing God.

It's as though the whole of life is now in colour, after being in black and white. We see the amazing love and creativity of God in all he has made—yes, and his sense of humour! We find a new appetite for living as the high walls of apathy are demolished. We want to join in with God—suffering where he suffers, and rejoicing where he rejoices.

So the exciting mystery of the Christian life unfolds. In the eyes of a hostile world it is a life of crazy values: inside-out, upside-down, and back-to-front! To the Christian, it is the very thing Jesus was describing when he said:

If anyone wants to come with me, he must forget self, take up his cross every day, and follow me. For whoever wants to save his own life will lose it, but whoever loses his life for my sake will save it.

FROM MATTHEW'S GOSPEL

CHIEFLY OURSELVES

When God takes action to change the world, he starts with individuals.

And the change he makes in them is so radical that Jesus described it as nothing less than 'new birth'.

New birth is not a second physical birth. It is spiritual. Our physical birth came from our mother and father, but our spiritual birth comes from the Holy Spirit of God.

New birth is not a matter of trying harder, or turning over a new

Shalom

The world longs for peace

Not 'a bit of peace' like a mother needs after a day with clamouring children; nor even a period of peace, by which we mean the absence of war.

It is God's peace we need. The Jews call it 'Shalom': a positive, restful and creative state of harmony. A settled society in which individuals are fulfilled, communities are integrated, and enemies are reconciled.

The need is urgent

The ideologies of both East and West have failed to deliver the perfect societies they promise.

Politicians, scientists and doctors wield immense power, but don't know which way to turn for guidelines on how to use it. Despite congresses, consultations and reports, a paralyzing greed keeps North rich and South poor.

Everyone, one way or another, is confronted by questions of *meaning*. What are the attitudes and values which will give new life?

The Christian answer is that God's peace comes from God.

It is this highly relevant, and all-pervading peace which Jesus came to establish.

It is the peace of the kingdom of God.

leaf. That would be like trying to give birth to ourselves, and it can't be done. New birth is something which comes entirely from God.

Nor is new birth a personality change. We probably appear very much the same as we did before, except that we have changed our mind about God. And from our new mind-set, new attitudes, habits, and goals will flow. Jesus described the signs of new birth in terms of the wind—invisible, but obviously and powerfully present.

When we come to Christ, and are born again, a new life begins in the

The gift of new life is given openly and freely by God. By accepting this gift, we can begin to experience life in all its fullness.

midst of the old world.

We become part of God's new creation—the kingdom of God which began to break in with Jesus, and is now turning the old order inside-out.

We are given the gift of the Holy Spirit, and become precious and indispensable members of the real church.

And we have an answer to the Big Questions:

- **Where am I?**
  I am in God's world.

- **Who am I?**
  I am God's child.

- **Why am I?**
  I have been made by God to know him and enjoy him for ever.

- **Is there a God?**
  Yes. And Jesus his Son is my Saviour and Lord.

Picture acknowledgments
Susanna Burton 49; Cephas Picture Library
(Franck Auberson) 37, (Stuart Boreham) 66
(bottom), (Jim Loring) 41, 66 (top), (Mick Rock)
66 (middle); Comstock 90; The Image Bank
(G. & V. Chapman) 42, 77, 89, (Terje Rakke)
64 (right), (Alex Stewart) 7; Lion Publishing
17, 19 (bottom), 22, 29, 51, (British Museum)
26, (David Townsend) 13, 53, 57; Nicholas Rous
19 (top), 64 (left), 65 (right); Peter Stiles (Val
Foster) 33; Tony Stone Images (Mel Lindstrom)
15, (David Madison) 47, (Philip & Karen Smith)
94, (Arthur Tilley) 25, (Roger Tully) 9;
Telegraph Colour Library (C. Franklin) 78/79,
(VCL) 8; ZEFA 20, 65 (left), (D. Falconer) 31,
(Jon Feingersh) 70, (Francekevich) 74, (Larry
Gilpin) 61, (L. Kemper) 79, (Koblmueller) 72/73,
(Ron Lowery) 10/11, (Starfoto) 28.